WORLD FAMOUS
CATASTROPHES

WORLD FAMOUS
CATASTROPHES

Ian Schott

SIENA

This is a Siena Book
Siena is an imprint of Parragon Book Service Ltd
Produced by Magpie Books, 1996

First published by Magpie Books
an imprint of Robinson Publishing Ltd, 1992
Robinson Publishing Ltd
7 Kensington Church Court
London W8 4SP

Copyright © Robinson Publishing 1992

Illustrations courtesy of Popperfoto
Cover picture: Herald of Free Enterprise, Topham,
Fires raging in downtown Kobe, Associated Press/Topham

A copy of the British Library Cataloguing in Publication Data is
available from the British Library

ISBN 0 75251 628 0

Printed and Bound in the EC

Contents

Catastrophes

Contents

Chapter One

On a Wing and a Prayer

A ir is one of the safest ways to travel; the statistics prove it. *You are far more likely to be run over than to plunge to your death from 30,000 feet. But the thought of this remains one of the traveller's deepest fears; and sometimes, accidents - and worse — do happen.*

The Lockerbie Christmas Horror

T he implication of a nut or bolt missing may be lost on passengers; but everybody has nightmares about bombs.

On 1 December, 1988, at 6.25 p.m., Pan Am flight 103 took off from Heathrow. It had originated in Frankfurt, Germany and was scheduled to fly to JFK Airport in New York, and from there to Detroit. In London, the passengers from Frankfurt had been switched from a three-engined Boeing 727 to a larger, four-engined 747. Amidst their baggage came a suitcase, without an owner. More passengers joined the flight at Heathrow. All included, there were two hundred and fifty-nine passengers and crew on board, many of them American students and military personnel travelling home to their families for Christmas. It was a happy flight.

The flight was running about twenty-five minutes late; Heathrow is busy at that time of year. Within fifty-two

A piece of the tail section of the Pan Am 747 which crashed at Lockerbie being lifted by an RAF helicopter.

minutes of take off, the aircraft was cruising in the winter darkness at 31,000 feet, twenty miles northwest of Carlisle, over the twinkling lights of the small, Scottish town of Lockerbie.

The bomb they had on board was tucked away inside a radio cassette player within that anonymous suitcase, deep in the baggage compartment. It was made of a plastic explosive called Semtex. Odourless and putty-like, this is near impossible to detect. Dogs can't smell it, and it can be moulded into any shape to fool the X-ray machine. A souvenir; the fabric of a dress, the lining of a suitcase. It probably had two detonators as insurance. The initial detonator was activated when the aircraft climbed above five thousand feet, shortly after it took off from Heathrow. This activated a timing device. For the last fifty minutes the fate of the passengers had been sealed. Then, an electric circuit closed, and ignited the blasting cap buried in the explosive.

The radar operator at Prestwick saw the single blip he was tracking suddenly turn into a shower of dots. Then these, too, disappeared.

Flight 103 had been blown apart. So high and fast was it moving, that the debris was sprayed over an area ten miles long and eighty miles wide. Most of the heavy metal and fuel rained onto the town of Lockerbie, engulfing it in a fireball, wrecking houses and leaving huge craters in the ground. Eleven of the inhabitants died. There was no hope of anyone surviving from Flight 103. The search for the bodies which had fallen from the sky went on for weeks; they were, and some still are, scattered across forests, mountains, fields and lakes. The world saw harrowing pictures of the dead and their sad possessions littering the countryside; some even fell onto the roofs of houses. It was the worst airline disaster in British history.

It transpired that various warnings had been given of the likelihood of a terrorist attack, but were thought to be hoaxes. Three years after this tragic murder, the British police announced that they were issuing arrest warrants for two Libyan officials to whom they said the long trail led. Many of the relatives of those who died are not satisfied with this explanation; they think the net went much wider, and want the truth.

"God help us – Goodbye" – the Japan Air Lines Catastrophe

In spite of constant vigilance, cracks in aircraft and faults due to bad maintenance still happen. When overlooked, the smallest problem inevitably turns into a killer. In 1978, a Japan Airlines 747 had a minor accident, and bashed its tail upon the ground when it landed. Incorrect repairs were made and passed without proper checks. Seven years later, this blunder came home to roost.

On 12 August, 1985, soon after take off, pressurized air leaked into the tail through the cracks which had spread like cancer through the rear bulkhead throughout those years. Inside the tail, it destroyed the sensitive rudder controls. The pilot discovered that the aircraft was not responding to

In March 1974, a Turkish Airline DC-10, carrying three hundred and forty-six passengers crashed on the outskirts of Paris. Everybody was killed. The cause was traced to a cargo door which came off in mid-air, causing massive decompression. This had nearly happened two years before to another DC-10. it was a design fault, but no-one had taken it seriously.

Firemen carrying a stretcher with the body of one of the victims of the Lockerbie crash past the remains of the jumbo jet's cockpit.

his commands. There were five hundred and twenty-four people on board. For the next thirty-two minutes they endured terror beyond belief as the aircraft dived and circled of its own accord. It finally swept into a remote mountain-side fifty-eight miles away. There were some survivors, but so dreadfully did the emergency services handle the crisis, squabbling over whose responsibility the rescue was, by the time help arrived it was fifteen hours after the crash. There were only four survivors. One of them, a stewardess, described the "screaming panic" on board. In the midst of this hell, some had written a last message to their families;

5

"To my three kids; take care of your mother. The aircraft is nose-diving. There is no hope. It was a happy life for me. Thank you all. God help us - goodbye."

Terror on the Tarmac – the Worst of them All

Tenerife, 27 March, 1977. The normally sunny holiday resort was covered by a shroud of mist and fog. Spring is one of the peak times for tourists, and the airport was under pressure. To make matters dramatically worse, a bomb had been found at neighbouring Las Palmas Airport, which had been closed. All traffic was being diverted to Tenerife, which was not equipped to deal with the situation. One of the aircraft diverted from Las Palmas was a Pan Am 747, originating from Los Angeles. It had three hundred and ninety-six passengers and crew. The aircraft sat at Tenerife, waiting for Las Palmas to re-open. Also at Tenerife, and also bound for Las Palmas, was another huge 747, this one operated by KLM. It had come from Amsterdam carrying two hundred and forty-eight passengers and crew. A total of six hundred and forty-four travelling to Las Palmas.

After a couple of hours delay, the aircraft were told that Las Palmas was now open; they could proceed to take off. They taxied down the run-way, the KLM 747 first. The Captain of the Pan Am flight was told to follow, but to take the third turning on the left off the strip and wait until the KLM 747 had taken off. When the KLM flight reached the end of the runway, it was to turn around and begin take-off. The Pan Am flight had to be safely out of the way.

When the aircraft had landed, visibility had been good. Now fog had settled over the airport. The pilots were following instructions from the control tower; nobody could see anybody else and the airport did not have a ground radar system.

What followed was a shameful catalogue of blind error and rashness. Whilst the Pan Am flight wandered down the runway in some confusion, looking for the third turning on the left, the KLM Flight, captained by the company's Chief Pilot Training Officer, reached the end of the runway and rapidly completed its pre-flight checks. He was in a hurry. Without waiting for correct clearance from the control tower, the Captain began to slowly move the aircraft forward. Meanwhile, in the fog the Pan Am flight were uncertain as to how many turnings they had passed. The third one seemed to be a long time coming. Unknown to them, they had missed it, and were taxiing towards disaster. At six minutes past five, as the KLM jet gathered speed, the Control Tower was certain it was still stationary, and had no intention of letting it go until he knew the Pan Am flight was off the runway and told them to let him know when they were clear. This exchange was relayed in the cabin of the KLM flight. The Captain ignored it. One of the KLM's crew, the engineer, hearing the conversation between the control tower and the Pan Am Flight, ventured to mention his doubts to his superior:

KLM Engineer: "Is he not clear, that Pan American?"

KLM Captain: "Oh yes!"

Eight seconds later the Pan Am saw the KLM Flight rushing towards them. The Pilot screamed:

"There he is ... look at him! Goddam! That-son-of-a-bitch is coming!"

The KLM crew tried to pull their aircraft up and over the Pan Am airplane. They just got off the ground, but the main landing gear smashed a path through the fuselage of the Pan Am airplane, and after five hundred feet of flight, it fell back onto the runway, slid another 1,000 feet and burst into flames incinerating everyone inside. The crushed and

7

Two top football teams have been decimated by air disasters. In February 1958 at Munich airport, most of the world-beating Manchester United team, whose average age was barely twenty, died in a crash precipitated by icy weather conditions. Peru lost six international players in 1987 when an aircraft carrying its leading club, Alianza Lima, plunged into the Pacific. A total of twenty-eight players died.

twisted metal of the Pan Am Aircraft trapped the surviving passengers; then a fire broke out.

Out of that six hundred and forty-four only fifty-nine survived, and they were all injured.

Britain's worst tarmac tragedy came in August 1985, at Manchester Airport, when the port engine on a British Airtours Boeing 727 exploded. The aircraft had been fitted with more seats than it was designed for, which clogged the exits. Fifty-four people died in the ensuing panic.

The End of the Airships

Air disasters have not been restricted to aircraft. Although considerably fewer people died in the great airship disasters in the 1930s, the sight of seven million cubic feet of hydrogen going up in flames put an end to the airship as a credible form of public transport.

The first fatalities were on board the British R101 in 1930. This was a government-built airship, and during its construction the Air Minister, Lord Thompson; had been very put out by the success of its sister ship, the R100. He

The burned out skeleton of the R101 airship near Beauvais, France, 1930.

laid considerable emphasis on the need for the R101 to succeed commercially, and announced that after completion it would be leaving for India on the 4th of October with himself on board. There, above the Indian continent, he would entertain Royalty and Government officials. The airship's quarters were suitably furnished in anticipation of the occasion. The dining facilities were packed with potted plants, 600 feet of Axminster carpet and heavy silver cutlery. Although there were only six passengers, no baggage restrictions were placed on them. Lord Thompson's luggage weighed as much as twenty-four people. There were forty-eight crew, mostly cooks and stewards.

The airship's vast frame contained seventeen hydrogen-filled gas-bags made, as there were no synthetics available, from stitched bullocks' intestines. These had a tendency to leak. The airship could only move at 71mph and weighed

The Hindenburg bursts into flames at Lakehurst, New Jersey, 1937.

twenty-three tons. The experts thought her underpowered and heavily weighed down by Lord Thompson's trappings. He would not be put off, declaring the ship "safe as houses, save for the millionth chance".

On 4 October, R101 shuddered laboriously into the sky and, scraping its way over treetops and church steeples, made for France. Once they left their moorings, these whales could not make an emergency landing. They had to go on. A resident of Hitchin outside London, alerted by a strange green and red light in her garden, ran outside to see the monster advancing at roof level up her street. The glare came from its coloured landing lights. Miraculously, it cleared the street, its vast belly bumping on roofs and knocking off chimneys. It just made it to France, where, at around 2.08 a.m., it hit a

The blazing Hindenburg sinks to the ground.

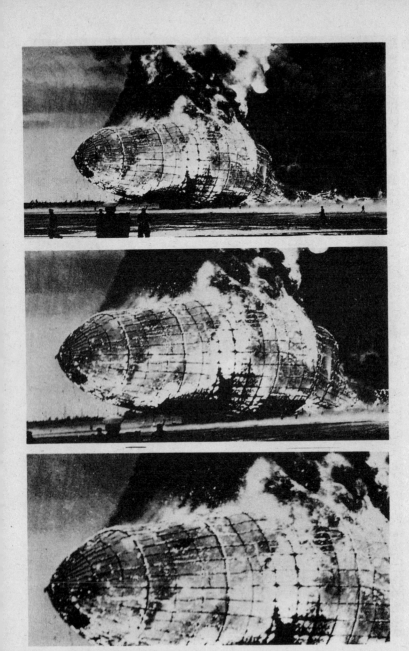

The Hindenburg ablaze.

low hill outside Beauvais and immediately burst into flames. There were no survivors.

Seven years later, the German airship Hindenburg, which proudly carried the Nazi swastika as it ferried passengers from Frankfurt to New York and back, met a similar fate. It was an absolute monster, nearly 800 feet long, a vast floating sausage which never failed to make an impression on people. With its superior engineering and ingenious design, it was a mobile advertisement for the Nazis.

On 3 May, 1937, it left Frankfurt and was set to dock at the Lakehurst mooring site outside New York at about 7.35 p.m. on the evening of the sixth. This wasn't its first trip, and there was only a little interest from the press. A couple of reporters turned up. One of them was Herb Morris, a young man working for a local radio station. He was given a portable tape recorder and told to describe the landing for possible broadcast later, if it seemed interesting enough. His commentary became legendary, because, as the leviathan docked, his patient description changed dramatically in tone:

". . . it's flashing, it's flashing, flashing terribly. Oh my God, it's bursting into flames! . . ."

Considering the heat generated by the burning of those millions of feet of hydrogen, it was remarkable that only thirty-six of the ninety-seven passengers died.

Two Shot Down

On 1 September 1983, a Soviet Fighter shot down a South Korean Airliner flying from New York to Seoul. Flight 007 had strayed off course, according to the Soviet Airforce, and in spite of being fitted with three separate navigational devices, was flying over the Kamchatka Peninsula and Sakhalin Island, where the Soviets had a heavy concentration of strategic naval bases. The pilot who shot it down

Catastrophes

When you think how overcrowded the skies currently are, it is surprising that collisions are a rarity, and that the worst one was thirty-two years ago in December 1960. Two aircraft carrying a total of one hundred and twenty-seven people collided over New York in a snow-storm. There was only one survivor. One of the aircraft fell onto Brooklyn, killing eight residents. By a miracle, it missed a school where 1,700 children were studying.

claimed that it did not respond to signals or warnings. On board were two hundred and sixty-nine passengers and crew, all of whom died. They included sixty-one Americans. President Reagan condemned it as a "horrifying act of violence".

Five years later, America was drawn into the war between Iran and Iraq, ostensibly to protect shipping passing through the Gulf. At the beginning of July 1988, the American destroyer Vincennes shot down an Iranian airliner with two hundred and ninety passengers on board. There were no survivors. The Vincennes mistakenly identified the big airliner as a small, hostile fighter plane.

Chapter Two

The Violent Earth ·

N othing inspires superstition and apocalyptic religious thought quite as much as an earthquake. The Bible speaks of them as being an instrument of God's wrath, and in all religions at all times they have been considered a sign of divine power. One marked the the death of Jesus we are told, and the Second Coming will be announced by many more.

The theory that the Earth's crust is composed of large segments or plates which move, has provided an explanation as to why earthquakes are more frequent in some places than others. The Japanese Islands, Southern Europe and the West Coast of America are particularly susceptible to earthquakes, being situated between plates, on "faults". The most notorious fault in the Western World is the San Andreas fault, which passes through the State of California. San Francisco suffered one of the world's most famous 'quakes early this century. For years they have been awaiting another devastating blow.

The power of earthquakes is measured on the Richter Scale, named after Charles Richter from the Californian Institute of Technology. The scale runs from 0-9. The smallest perceptible 'quake has a magnitude of 2. The most destructive have a magnitude of more than 8. Such 'quakes release an amount of energy greater than 10,000 Atomic bombs of the type dropped on Hiroshima. Even modest earthquakes can produce twenty-foot faults in the Earth; surface cracks ten feet wide open up and swallow whatever is above. Fences, roads and houses can move several feet if they have not been destroyed. Earthquakes cause bridges to collapse, dams to burst, create landslides, avalanches and most terrible of all, "tsunami" - the seismic waves wrongly called tidal waves. Sparked off by the shock waves from *earthquakes, the centres of which are often miles under the surface of the ocean, mountains of water sixty-foot high strike coastal districts at speeds of 250mph. Tsunami are the destroyers of cities and islands.*

Ancient Earthquakes

Perhaps the most destructive earthquake ever was that which struck the Eastern Mediterranean on 21 July, AD 365. It hit Italy, Greece, Syria, Palestine and Egypt. Alexandria in Egypt, one of the jewels of the Roman Empire, was devastated. The 600-foot lighthouse, one of the Wonders of the World, visible for thirty miles, fell into the harbour. A vast seismic wave sped in and deposited ships on the roofs of houses miles away from the sea. Antioch in Syria suffered frequently from earthquakes in ancient times. In AD 526, 250,000 lost their lives in a severe shock. At another time, the Roman Emperor Trajan who was staying in the city only escaped death by scrambling out of a window before the house he was in collapsed. There were no instruments for scientific prediction of earthquakes, so people were reliant on prophecy and astrology. These methods of divining the future, still popular among American Presidents, were resorted to in California in the Sixties and Seventies, so great was the fear of a 'quake. An astrologer apparently got it right at Tabriz in Iran, AD 1042. Sadly, the astrologer's message was not welcome at the time. No-one took him seriously and 40,000 died. An awful earthquake hit three huge provinces of China in the sixteenth century. From the area affected, it was estimated that at least 800,000 were killed.

The Straits of Messina, between the toe of Italy and the coast of Sicily, are the legendary lair of the mythic monsters, Scylla and Charybdis, who sat either side of the water and devoured passing ships. The area is notorious for earthquakes, which send seismic waves rushing on to both shores. Reggio de Calabria was destroyed on the Italian coast in 1509 and 1638, on which occasion 10,000 died. In 1693, north and eastern Sicily were struck by a 'quake that killed 93,000. In more recent times both sides of the Straits were hit by a terrible earthquake in 1908. On 28 December, at 5.10 a.m., there was a slight tremor. Ten minutes later, a deep rumbling began, and the waters of the Straits began to stir, as if shaken by those mythic monsters. The vibrations grew in severity and spread out towards the coasts of Italy and Sicily. Reggio, Messina and all coastal villages were reduced to rubble. Meanwhile, the sea sucked back until it was fifty yards clear of the shore, and then swept back in a twenty-foot high wave that completed the destruction. The intensity of the 'quake was staggering; in some towns, there was not a building left standing, and 160,000 were dead.

An interesting feature of this 'quake was its early morning start. Earthquakes are early risers, and much of the loss of life that occurs is due to their ability to catch whole populations in their beds.

The San Francisco Earthquake

On Wednesday, 18 April, 1906, at the earthquake's favourite time, shortly after 5 a.m., the inhabitants of San Francisco (population 340,000) heard a long and ominous rumbling, like the sound of thunder, or the distant cracking of timber. Within a few seconds, they felt the first tremor. There were six in total. By the worst and third at 8.45 a.m., everyone was awake. The shocks threw people out of bed and out of windows in some cases. One man later told how he had watched a massive, heavy wardrobe in his bedroom

Catastrophes

On 7 June, 1692, the Caribbean slaving and trade centre of Port Royal, Jamaica was wrecked and drowned by an earthquake and wave. It was another sweltering morning in the town whose occupants, pirates, slave traders and pimps were thought to be "the most ungodly people under the sun". At 11.47 a.m., as the inhabitants went about their business, the port was hit by three almost simultaneous shocks, which brought the houses down. Then, from out of the calm, blue sea, came an enormous tsunami. It rolled in and submerged the town forever. Even the dead did not escape. A surviving clergyman wrote:

"It is a sad sight to see this harbour, one of the fairest I ever saw, covered with the dead of people of all conditions, floating up and down without burial; for the burial place was destroyed by the earthquake which shook to pieces the tombs, and the sea washed the carcasses of those who had been buried out of their graves . . ."

The port now lies under water at the entrance to Kingston Harbour. It is said that the houses can be seen under the sea, and the ghostly ringing of church bells is often heard.

tip over at near right angles several times, each time swinging vertical again before it was tossed forward and smashed. Throughout the city, furniture danced around the houses, and there was not a cup, plate or glass that was not smashed. This was superficial. Then, buildings which had been bumping up and down started to collapse. One man awoke in his boarding-house to see the leg of a child coming through a hole which had appeared in his ceiling. Then the vibrations squeezed the gap closed, and the leg was snipped off and fell on him. He leapt out of the window as the building crumbled.

When the heaviest shock hit, the urban landscape shook as if it were boiling. It rose up and down as if tossed on waves. Where there had been hotels, tenements and mansions there was only rubble. Houses still standing leant at 15° from the vertical. The new $7 million Palace Hotel was wrecked. One of its guests was the legendary singer, Enrico Caruso, who vowed never to come back to San Francisco. Buildings split down the middle from cornice to foundation. The 'quake-proof City Hall collapsed. The roads disappeared. The wharves cracked. Amazingly, amid the devastation, there were only 1,000 casualties. The earlier shocks had given people the opportunity to leave

San Francisco's City Hall after the earthquake in 1906.

buildings which subsequently fell down. Martial law was declared and soldiers shot four looters. Then, fire sparked off by gas leaks broke out.

Damage from the earthquake did not compare with that caused by the fire. It swept the business district, and wind carried it to other parts of the already chaotic city. Eight square miles comprising several hundred blocks of buildings were totally burned out. Nearly 250,000 were left homeless. The damage was estimated at $250 million. San Francisco was a smouldering ruin.

Its recovery was no less dramatic. Within three years, while thousands lived in tents, a third of the city was rebuilt on earthquake and fire resistant lines. In 1911, to mark its extraordinary rejuvenation, San Francisco was chosen to host a world fair. Tidal land was reclaimed on which to build a 650-acre site featuring landscaped gardens, palaces and pavilions. It opened in 1915 and had nineteen million visitors; San Francisco had literally risen from the ashes.

The Tokyo Earthquake

On Saturday, 1 September 1923, a powerful shock hit Tokyo and the port of Yokahama, eight miles to the southwest of the outer fringe of the city on the shore of Tokyo Bay. Shocks of a minor nature had been felt in the region since time immemorial, situated as it is near the Pacific trench called the "Tuscarora Deep". Building methods had been adapted accordingly. There were a few Western-style concrete structures in Tokyo, but the majority of the city was still a huge village of one-storey houses built out of light-weight materials like timber and thatch. Even the beams in the houses could be dismantled at the threat of a tremor, so that whole structures could be taken apart and put back together again when the danger was passed.

Not all waves are water. On 15 January 1919, a fifty-foot high tank of molasses (black treacle) owned by the Purity Distilling Company exploded in Boston USA. Twenty people were killed and forty injured as a fifteen-foot high wave of treacle surged through the commercial district of the city. The sticky killer swamped houses and buried a fire-station.

This time, however, the precautions were in vain. As so often, there were three shocks. All were equally massive, and after the earthquake came the fire. The city collapsed instantly. As the earth buckled, parts of it were raised ten foot, and at others the ground opened up and swallowed pedestrians, vehicles and houses. The business quarter and most government offices were razed. A power station collapsed killing six hundred outright. The Tokyo arsenal blew up, further inspiring the flames that damage to the gas and electricity systems had created. Japan's longest tunnel at Sasako caved in on train passengers. All bridges disintegrated. The Prime Minister was holding a cabinet meeting when the floor gave way and twenty of his colleagues were killed. Sagami Bay was struck by forty-foot waves. Tokyo had been a cultural and religious centre for 4,000 years. Seventeen libraries were destroyed, besides six hundred and forty Buddhist temples and one hundred and fifty Shinto shrines. In the modern port of Yokohama, the American Hospital, the two major hotels, the quays, the pier and innumerable lesser buildings collapsed, the Hospital falling into the bay. The massive oil storage tanks in the harbour were ripped open, and the thousands of people who poured down to the port hoping to escape by sea were greeted by the sight of a wall of blazing oil advancing across the ocean

Catastrophes

> "Mexico has been hit with the force of a mighty blow from hell" is how one witness described the scene, after an earthquake measuring 8.1 on the Richter scale struck Mexico City at 7.20 a.m. on 19 September, 1985. The centre of the 'quake was actually two hundred and forty-eight miles away, under the sea-bed of the Pacific Ocean. As a consequence, sixty-foot high tsunami crashed into the coast at phenomenal speeds. Large areas of the city "pancaked", the multi-storey, cheaply built tenements and office blocks deflating, one floor falling down onto the next beneath it. Government officials put the death-toll at 4,500, a figure which grossly underestimated the carnage for political reasons and which was ridiculed by aid workers who thought it nearer 40.000.

towards them. In Yokohama, fire broke out almost simultaneously with the shocks. In Tokyo, it gathered to a peak of ferocity that saw 40,000 people burned to death in a maelstrom in Tokyo Park. Many were snatched up by the fire-cyclone and their incinerated bodies deposited hundreds of yards away. Those who tried to survive by standing head high in the canals were later found with their heads charred beyond recognition; the fire had swept along the surface of the water.

In the grisly aftermath, it was calculated that 150,000 had died. Over 700,000 private dwellings were destroyed. Now, seventy years later, Tokyo and its surrounding area is the most thickly populated region in Japan. Tremors are still felt; it is entirely likely that Tokyo can expect another serious earthquake in the future.

The Second Great Chinese Earthquake

After having endured the single most destructive earthquake recorded in terms of human life in 1556, China endured an horrific repetition four hundred and twenty years later in 1976. This time, two shocks, fifteen hours apart, were responsible for somewhere between 700,000

The young and unsettled mountain region of South and Central America has had a history of violent disturbances. In the 1970s, a string of earthquake disasters came within a period of six years. Principal among these was the 7.75 shock of 31 May 1970 in Peru. This insidious shock struck when most of the soccer-mad population were indoors listening to the World Cup on their radios. Sparked by the 'quake, a dam burst, and swept away the towns of Yungay and Caras with their population of 80,000. Many villages ceased to exist. After the shock and the flood, 66,794 were dead or missing. Another million were injured or homeless.

In December 1972, Managua, the Nicaraguan capital, suffered over two hundred shocks in two terrible days that left 7,000 dead. One rather unexpected inhabitant was billionaire Howard Hughes, being reclusive as usual, who quickly fled somewhere safer and less conspicuous. The 'quakes left 300,000 homeless. Four years later, In February 1976, a 7.5 shock struck Guatemala and the Honduras, killing 22,000.

Catastrophes

and 1.4 million deaths. The Chinese did not make the death toll official. The shocks, the first of which occurred at 3.40 a.m. on 28 July (the earthquake once again catching everybody in bed), measured 8.2 and 7.9 on the Richter scale. These two shocks released a destructive energy the equivalent of 20,000 World War II Atomic bombs, or 400 million tons of high explosive. The "epicentre" of the 'quake was at T'angshan, a city with a million inhabitants. The urban centres of Peking and Tientsin were also badly affected. T'angshan, however, was ruined. Two thirds of the city was lost to the earthquake, with 655,000 deaths. Those who visited the city, months after said there was only twenty miles of rubble left.

The tremors from the Chinese catastrophe were felt 3,500 miles away in Alaska. This sparsely populated area of the world has the distinction of having experienced the most violent earthquake recorded, although, due to the remote nature of the region, only thirty-one died. On Good Friday, 1964, with a shock factor that nearly went off the Richter scale, 49 million, 420,000 acres of Alaskan landscape was lifted up by at least a meter and then dropped again.

Chapter Three

Hell on Wheels

The statistics regarding death on the roads are mind-boggling. While we are shocked or awed by the casualty figure from a single major catastrophe or a war, all around us there is an unrelenting massacre going on. In the United States, automobiles are the number five killer, with nearly twenty-one deaths per 100,000 of the population, a higher rate than diabetes, and heart problems. Cars are responsible for more deaths than suicide and murder combined. During the Vietnam War, 46,000 Americans were killed. During the same period, 653,000 Americans died on the roads. In the final year of the Vietnam conflict, 54,000 Americans died in automobile related accidents. Cars are killers, more so than any disease.

In Britain, the worst single crash remains the M6 pile-up on a foggy morning in 1971, near Liverpool. Cars travelling too fast and too close formed an enormous two hundred car string of wrecks. Ten people died. In March of 1991, there was a similar smash on the M4 in Berkshire, in which ten also died and twenty-five were injured.

Motorized Killers

Much of the destruction in mass pile-ups is due to explosions and fire. Fuel tankers and other highly inflammable cargoes travelling at high speed are potential bombs.

In Tortosa, Spain, in 1978 one of the worst accidents of this type happened. It was on 8 July, a scorching hot day. A

25

Catastrophes

> Poona, India; May 1975. An ever-loaded truck
> carrying eighty guests to a wedding was struck
> by a train which killed sixty-nine people.

tanker carrying a thirty-eight ton load of liquid propylene gas was travelling down the coast road, which would take it past a crowded beach-side campsite. Here, nearly five hundred people were holidaying, spread out over the camp-site and beach in caravans and tents. Because of a blow-out, or maybe because the driver fell asleep, the tanker careered off the road into the centre of the camp. The impact broke open the tank and instantaneously the camp-site was engulfed by a fireball. The explosion triggered a chain reaction, setting off dozens of smaller explosions as the gas-cylinders people were using for cooking blew up, and then the fuel-tanks of cars. So fierce was the heat that a discotheque across the road spontaneously exploded into flames. The tanker's blast left a sixty foot crater, fifteen foot deep.

Campers were blown hundreds of feet, some landing well out to sea; some were buried by sand; many were never found. The bodies that were recovered were burned beyond recognition. Over one hundred and fifty died, and hundreds were injured.

In a similar incident on 25 May, 1950 in Chicago, Illinois, a tanker carrying 8,000 gallons of gasoline ploughed into a rush-hour tram when the traffic signals failed. In the

> South Korea, 14 October 1970. A train struck a
> bus carrying schoolboys on a midweek
> excursion. The fuel tank of the bus ruptured and
> fifty-two boys were killed.

resulting heat, buildings close by caught fire. The windows
in those further away melted; concrete and bricks buckled
and collapsed. Thirty-four people died.

Quite the most catastrophic accident of this nature -
though it was later claimed by the Government that it was
sabotage – occurred in Cali, Columbia in 1956. Shortly after
midnight on 7 August, a military convoy containing several
tons of fuel, explosives and ammunition, blew up as it
passed through the centre of town. Eight blocks of the city
around the blast were razed; windows in houses three miles
away were shattered; 1,200 people were killed, and thousands injured.

Chapter Four

Natural Killers

A ny of the natural killers have now been largely eradicated from the Western World. Tuberculosis, typhus, cholera, diphtheria, chicken-pox and measles no longer take away large sections of the population in their youth, and few in the West will starve to death. Within a century, average life expectancy in the West has doubled as a consequence of improved sanitary conditions, better diet and the discovery of vaccines. Now genetic engineers in America believe that they have their hands on the cogs and gears of the ageing process itself, and see no reason why, under the right circumstances, it should not be possible for a human being to live for 200,000 years. The real effects of this will be felt within a very short time; the American government is pouring billions into research aimed at prolonging the lives of its huge elderly population. For those who wish, and can afford it, an eternal and utterly meaningless life looks increasingly possible. There will be nothing remotely interesting about such a desperate, selfish and old world, inhabited and ruled by the ageless wealthy. In developing and Third World nations, disease, drought, famine, civil war, poverty, over population and crippling debt to Western banks continue to be responsible for death on a cataclysmic scale.

*　　*　　*

Plagues and Pestilence

T he single most devastating killer remains the Black Death, bubonic plague, which swept across Europe between 1347 and 1350. This killed a quarter of the population - twenty-five million - and, in one form or another, continued to re-emerge, though less virulently, for the next five hundred years. Its spread changed the face of the known world.

Bubonic plague was first historically recorded in about the third century AD in the Middle East. In AD 542, it erupted in Egypt, spread to Constantinople, where it killed 10,000 in a day, and within a few years was in France. It is quite possible that it paid a visit to England in the seventh century. Its characteristic signs were red eyes, a swollen tongue, convulsive vomiting, splitting headaches, and horribly inflamed glands, or buboes, in the groin. The skin of victims turned dark in patches - hence the name "Black Death".

Incubation took a mere four to six days and the mortality rate for the early outbreaks was ninety-nine per cent. People died in excruciating agony, rambling and staggering incoherently. Its principal means of travel were fleas carried by black rats, squirrels and other rodents. In Summer, when the fleas thrived, so did the plague.

In the fourteenth century, a particularly virulent strain began its procession westwards. It is thought to have originated in China and the Far East. The Chinese army actually used plague-ridden corpses as weapons, catapulting them into besieged cities. About thirteen million died in China.

The plague was then carried by travellers, rats on ships and the Tartar and Mongol armies into Europe. An Italian lawyer, Gabriel de Mussis, accompanied the march of the plague, as he journeyed from the Crimea to Genoa in Italy, and watched his band of fellow travellers gradually diminish and die. It is also thought that the black rat returned from the East with the Crusaders. Italy was the first European country to suffer. From there it was carried to Spain, France, Britain, Central Europe and Scandinavia.

There was nothing people could do except pray and watch it spread. Overcrowded villages and appalling sanitary conditions in cities helped the plague. Whole communities were wiped out and corpses clogged the streets or were hurled over the walls of towns; often there was no-one left to bury them. Families broke up, social structures disintegrated, crime soared. In vain the wealthy hid in their manor-houses and castles. The flea found them. As there was no-one to work the fields, famine followed. Education came to a halt as teachers died. The Continent was plunged into darkness.

In the wake of the plague, social unrest spread; there were peasant uprisings and bitter fighting between survivors. There was also a dramatic increase in strange cults, in Satanic worship and in a morbid fascination for the grotesque, which has been passed down in painting, literature and folk-tales, to this day; the Black Death still remains part of the European consciousness.

Bubonic plague was never far away throughout the following three centuries. It continued to break out on the Continent, and in the Far East it was a perfectly usual way to die; plague continued to ravage India well into the twentieth century, though the mortality rate for sufferers fell steadily; having the plague no longer meant that one was going to automatically die. In 1900, there were outbreaks in places as far apart as Portugal and Australia. The most famous recurrence in Europe was the Great Plague of London in 1664-65. It came into the country, quite probably, from Holland, where there had been a nasty outbreak. Some contemporaries thought that a specific cargo of Dutch cloth carried the killer. In November 1664, a few isolated cases were noted in the parishes of

Advances in antibiotics mean that a dose of influenza is unlikely to turn into pneumonia. This is a comparatively recent development. At the conclusion of World War I, perhaps ten million had died on the battlefields of Europe. The combatants had come from three continents, and were crowded together in some of the most dreadful conditions ever known to man. These provided a perfect breeding ground for an influenza epidemic that they then re-exported and which circled an enfeebled Earth in 1918-19. War had weakened nations; the bug was vigorous. Within a year, twenty million had died.

St Giles and St Martins in the western side of London. Slowly at first, it spread eastwards to the populous heart of the old City of London. When Spring came, the plague gathered momentum. In May, 1665, forty-three died. In June, 6,137 died; in July, 17,036 and at its peak in August, 31,159 were killed by the plague. In all, a total of 68,596 - fifteen per cent of the population of London - died in that terrible Summer. It became customary to shut up the houses where the plague had broken out, incarcerating and condemning to death whole families. These houses were distinguished by a red cross painted on the door, and the words "God have mercy on us". Others barricaded themselves in to escape the plague; many fled. London became a ghost town. Shortly afterwards, the Great Fire swept away the narrow streets and wooden houses, and cleansed the city of the plague.

Recently some experts have speculated that AIDS could bring about a serious long-term decline in population numbers; within a few years, it could be killing more people than are born in some developing countries. In certain central African countries, HIV, the virus that causes AIDS, has infected up to thirty per cent of pregnant women. The true, devastating effects of AIDS are yet to come. It makes no exceptions and causes near one hundred per cent mortality.

Drought and Famine

These two horsemen of the Apocalypse are normally twins. Famine occurs when the normal food supply fails, usually due to below average rainfall over a period of years. Alternatively, above average rainfall can encourage over-cultivation and overpopulation by men and animals. When the climate changes, a catastrophe follows. The earth is a planet dependent on water. It carries with it through space a fixed amount, somewhere in the region of forty-five million cubic yards per person; the distribution of that water constantly changes according to climatic conditions.

Over-grazing, erosion, desertification caused by the removal of essential trees and shrubs, the cultivation of unsuitable land for supposedly lucrative "cash-crops", which poor countries are obliged to grow in order to feed their all devouring debts, all contribute. Recently, extensive civil war throughout much of Africa has caused an enormous refugee problem. Millions have been forcibly turned nomadic with no means of supporting or feeding themselves. The famine problem has been growing for the last twenty years. Throughout the African continent, there are potentially forty million at risk of acute deprivation. Elsewhere, Europe, America and Russia have all experienced the devastating effects of mass starvation following in the wake of war and depression. By the time you hear about a

In the good harvest of 1930, the Ukraine accounted for twenty-seven per cent of the Soviet Union's total grain production. But Stalin demanded that it should supply nearly forty per cent of Russian grain deliveries. He continued to demand that this figure, amounting to 7.7 million tons be supplied even when the harvest was poor in the following years. In 1932, over half the Ukraine's grain was being taken from it. Stalin refused to drop the quota demanded, and people began to starve whilst grain piled up and rotted in railway depots and warehouses under armed guard. What followed was tantamount to murder; Stalin wished to crush the peasants of the Ukraine. From 1933, famine became widespread. The Ukraine was cordoned off. There was no-one to garner the rotting crops; the countryside was reduced to a "melancholy desert" and five million died. Hearing about what he had done, Stalin's second wife shot herself.

famine it is generally too late to avert disaster. They have to be countered by planning and forethought.

Appalling famines have regularly occurred since history began. The Bible is full of them. In Egypt in 1064-72, the Nile failed to flood its banks for seven years. The Egyptians were dependent upon this to irrigate their crops. In the resulting famine, people resorted to cannibalism.

India has experienced many famines. During the reign of Shah Jahan, who built the Taj Mahal, a famine killed 30,000 in the city of Surat. Parents sold their children to obtain food. In the province of Bengal in 1769, a severe famine

Catastrophes

caused by drought killed somewhere between three to ten million people, a third of the population.

In 1876-79, both India and China suffered one of the worst famines ever. In India, the monsoon failed in the south and north in successive years; in the province of Madras alone, three and a half million died of starvation and disease. In China, no rain fell for three years. The outside world did not hear about the catastrophe for a year; and due to the remote nature of the communities, relief was near impossible. The only way to dispose of the bodies was in what were called "ten thousand man holes..". As with so many of the disasters that have afflicted China, precise figures for the numbers killed are impossible to come by. Estimates vary from nine to thirteen million or more.

From 1972, the West African drought and famine began in the area called the "sahel", the strip of land between the Sahara desert and the fertile lands to the south. It is an area stretching from the Atlantic Ocean, via Mauritania, Mali, Upper Volta, Niger, Chad to Senegal, Ghana, Nigeria, the Central African Republic and Ethiopia. It was a result of climatic change, ecological rape and incompetent political management. It could have been averted, but it ended up affecting twenty-five million Africans. Over-population and over-grazing had followed in the wake of eight good years; when the drought came, the cattle stripped the countryside and then eighty per cent of them died, clogging the river beds. Disease followed starvation and at least 200,000 died. There was no distribution network for the aid that arrived. The political turmoil that followed saw civil war break out. Niger's government fell, and Emperor Haile Selassie of Ethiopia departed.

In 1984, the continuing African famine which had not been a fashionable subject of conversation, came back into the public conscience as a result of TV reporting and the extraordinary fund-raising efforts of Bob Geldof and the Band-Aid record and concert, which raised £20 million. A

34

whole series of charity efforts followed, in spite of which a million died in Ethiopia. The scale of the problem can be gauged by the fact that Comic Relief recently raised £12 million for the Third World. They re-pay that sum every day in interest on their debts to Western banks.

The Killer Heat

In June, 1980, the temperature in America rocketed nationwide and stayed that way for the next two months. In Dallas, Texas, an astonishing twenty-three days with a temperature in excess of 100°F were recorded; within the first month, 1,200 people died. Crime soared. Cases of domestic violence and child abuse swelled dramatically. In the cities, hit in May by race-riots, there was more trouble. It became impossible to stay outside for any length of time without contracting heatstroke. At night, the temperature barely dropped into the eighties. In one night in Washington, it never dropped below 91°, with a humidity of eighty-five per cent; you would be cooler in a slow oven. Across America, states of emergency were declared as people collapsed in the streets. The Red Cross set up emergency relief centres and distributed fans. Air conditioning made the difference between life and death for many, which meant that most who died were in the poorer areas. People did not cook for weeks, and were too lethargic to leave their houses. The sun was too hot for all but insane tourists to lie in, so there was the remarkable sight of people queueing to use solariums in some of the hottest weather ever. The heat sparked off brush fires which devastated Arizona. Farmers lost $2 billion worth of crops and livestock. Companies, already in the throes of a recession were hit by massive absenteeism, as employees simply stayed indoors to escape the sun. It was not until August that the temperatures dropped to anywhere near approaching normal.

The Irish Potato Famine

This terrible famine might also be called "The famine that helped build America". It was as a consequence of it that so many of the Irish emigrated to the New World, and passed within the space of a few generations, from peasants to Presidents.

The humble potato was introduced into Europe from South America in the sixteenth and seventeenth centuries. By the middle of the nineteenth century it was grown throughout most of the continent as a supplement to other grain crops, appreciated for its basic nutritional value, but not over relied upon.

Ireland was ruled by the English, most notably by absentee English landlords. These, concerned only with the enhancement of their income, let the land they owned to agents, who in turn subdivided it further and let it in tiny plots in their pursuit of wealth. The result was that at least three million Irish farm labourers had less than a tenth of a hectare apiece on which to grow food for their families. With the exception of a tiny space for a mud cottage, the whole of this area would be used to grow potatoes. Two-thirds of the labourers' annual wage of a pitiful £7 was taken by the agent for rent of the cottage and land. The money left was not enough to feed a dog on, and only potatoes could provide enough carbohydrate to keep a family alive; day after day, month after month it was always the same menu.

Then in 1845, a fungus struck potato crops across Europe. They rotted in the ground. The strange mould on them was noted, but no-one thought it might be the cause of the catastrophe. Instead, they blamed the weather, witchcraft, God and the Devil. The fungus was later discovered to be a parasite which landed on the potato and cast a net of tiny little suckers by which it drained its goodness. It was not until thirty years after the famine struck Ireland that copper sulphate was found to prevent the parasite. In Ireland, the spores from the fungus had been spread far and wide by the strong winds that are a natural part of its climate.

For the Irish poor, it was a cataclysm. They had nothing to eat, and were reduced to foraging for berries and seaweed in their efforts to stay alive. There was an attempt by the English government to provide some relief in the form of grain, but as the famine persisted, typhus and dysentery added to the toll taken by starvation. Over a period of ten years, the population shrank from eight to five million. Not all had died; many had emigrated across the Atlantic, to where they were to have such a profound influence on the future of America.

Chapter Five

The Final Frontier

S purred on by the Cold War between Russia and America, the 1960s and 1970s were a triumphant time for space exploration. More than just being an assertion of a nation's technological powers and a piece of propaganda, exploration also expressed the aspirations of man; to go further, to know more and perhaps to reconcile national differences in acts of great symbolic value. Space exploration could ultimately be about shared human interests and therefore about peace. There were many scientific spin-offs; from the non-stick frying pan to computers, space-age technology entered everyone's lives. The aspirations were quite clear; the Moon, then Mars, then perhaps Jupiter; planetary exploration.

Exploring the Universe or Military Expansion?

T he first casualties of the hugely successful American programme came in 1967. On 27 January, astronauts Virgil Grissom, Edward White and Roger Chaffee died when a flash fire swept through their Apollo capsule during a simulated countdown. The three astronauts, who were rehearsing for a launch the following week, were burned alive in a fire made more intense by the one hundred per cent oxygen atmosphere in the cockpit. Pure oxygen was being used by the Americans in an attempt to lessen, even by a fraction of an ounce, the weight of the craft. An emergency crew managed to get to the craft within four minutes, but the capsule was hot enough to melt their skin. When they prised the door open, flames poured out, and they were forced to retreat. For the next two hours, until the heat cooled, unwilling spectators in the control centre could see the smouldering bodies of the astronauts on the closed circuit cameras, which had continued to relay the events.

In the next few years, the American space programme began to develop in another, tentative, direction. In 1972, President Nixon announced that the United States would be attempting to build a re-usable space-shuttle. In the meantime, the Apollo programme continued, and in July 1975, in a truly historic moment, American and Soviet spaceships docked in a gesture of international co-operation. When Ronald Reagan became President in 1980, promising a reborn nation dedicated to the 'preservation of liberty', the shuttle programme was well advanced and the following year the first craft, Columbia, one of a proposed fleet, made a successful touchdown in the California desert. It had circled the Earth thirty-six times in its flight of fifty-four hours, and the only problem had been the loss of a few ceramic tiles on the heat shield. It was intended to build up the number of shuttle flights to one a fortnight.

Reagan's policies meant a massive increase in defence spending, and a new era in the Cold War. Much faith was placed in advanced technology, which would eventually culminate in Reagan's 'Star Wars' plan - the Strategic Defence Initiative - in which he envisioned an umbrella of defensive systems in space which would 'zap' Russian missiles before they hit America. Reagan, who in his days as an actor had starred in films in which secret laser weapons shot down Communist aircraft, became infatuated by Edward Teller, the father of the most terrible weapon man has yet created, the Hydrogen Bomb. This extraordinary German, a refugee from the Nazis, was absolutely convinced that the nuclear conflict with the Soviet Union was inevitable; he assured Reagan that it would be possible for a laser the size of an executive desk to shoot down a thousand Russian missiles. This assertion was made after tests proving that nothing of the sort was on the cards; in all aspects of this research, money was used to try and buy results that at heart, people realized could only come in time, if ever. In 1992, after $25 billion of expenditure, that 'Star Wars' vision is a long way off fulfilment, the project sinking under accusations of fraud and corruption.

As a result of this hawkish attitude, and the personalities that began to dominate America's space programme, the shuttle programme began increasingly to be looked at from a military perspective. Furthermore, Reagan laid great emphasis on it as a symbol of American superiority and relished the photo-opportunities it offered. The programme also came under pressure to justify itself commercially, by launching satellites. Veterans, who for decades had worked with the simple objectives of exploration and the accumulation of knowledge, began to feel interfered with and confused. The confidence within NASA, the American space agency was further shaken when its boss, Jim Beggs, was indicted by the government on fraud charges and removed from his post; shortly afterwards the charges were dropped. His replacement was his former deputy, who had barely started at NASA. William Graham was an avid "Reaganite", who had previously specialized in US preparations for nuclear war. He brought a distinctly military slant to the organization, and made no secret of his views that American prestige versus the Russians must be boosted by the Space shuttle programme, and not by planetary exploration.

Hence the NASA scientists found themselves under acute pressure, and also uncertain what their objectives now were. The Space shuttle programme, costing half a billion dollars per flight, had to keep on performing to keep the money coming. In haste and doubt about the nature of the whole project, corners were cut, safety checks became sloppy. Whilst high level support for the programme was outspoken, linking it quite clearly to Reagan's patriotic 're-birth' of the nation, privately, morale was not so good. It wouldn't do to say so though. Reagan liked people who told him what he wanted to hear. A target of twenty-five flights a year was re-iterated by the management. Something was going to give.

On 28 January, 1986, the shuttle Challenger was on the launch pad for a trip that would see America's first schoolteacher in space. Christa McAuliffe, cheered on by many of her students, planned to use a live video link-up on the trip to motivate young people to work towards higher personal achievement. Apart from her, the shuttle had a crew of six astronauts, ranging in experience. Commander Dick Scobee had previously flown in the shuttle, as had the three mission specialists on board, who would supervise the launch of the shuttle's payload, a $100 million NASA satellite. The rest of the crew was made up of a hot-shot Navy Pilot, Michael Smith, whose first trip it was, and another, rookie astronaut. Between them, they represented three races and four religions. It was a very cold morning, colder than they would normally risk, as the rubber seals of the solid-fuel booster rockets had been known to fail in cold temperatures. But they were five days behind schedule, and as ever, the pressure to perform was on.

All shuttle launches were captured on powerful tracking cameras, in vivid colours, with the pictures fed live to TV networks. Millions were watching, as at 11.38 a.m., the Challenger lifted flawlessly off the launch pad at Cape Canaveral and headed up into the blue sky at a speed of 2,900 feet per second, trailing an immense tower of vapour. At a height of nine miles it was still clearly visible to all below. Commander Scobee gave the order to increase power, and then, seventy-three seconds into the flight,

Catastrophes

It came from outer space, hurtling into our atmosphere with the brightness of a second sun, and crashing into the earth in Siberia at 1.17 a.m. on 30 June, 1908. Nobody will ever truly know what it was, but the effects of the collision were unforgettable. Even in Washington, half a world away, the force was felt; the shock waves rippled twice around the earth. A pillar of fire, eleven miles high, leapt heaven-wards, and for days afterwards the night-skies over Europe glowed eerily. Four hundred and ninety-seven miles away, explosions were still deafening; for twenty-eight miles around the blast, the dense forest was burned and flattened. Whether asteroid, comet, meteor or alien space ship, its collision had the explosive force of several hydrogen bombs. It was a miracle it hit in such a remote area. There was no human for hundreds of miles, but it killed every other living thing. If it had fallen in the sea, it could have caused global flooding on an irreparable scale, with fifty-foot high seismic waves destroying every coastline for thousands of miles.

Bits of rock fall from space all the time. There's also a vast quantity of space-junk now floating around the earth. Well over 4,000 pieces of ex-satellites and discarded pieces of rocket. What goes up must come down; big objects already have fallen - Skylab for example - and smaller bits fall every day, so far safely, burning up on entering the Earth's atmosphere. There are dramatic things on the horizon. A few years ago, a Russian scientist predicted that a very large asteroid will strike Earth within the next twenty-five years. To give an idea of the catastrophe that might bring about, it's worth considering the latest theories as to why the dinosaurs disappeared. The dinosaurs roamed the earth for more than one hundred million years. Then, in what scientists describe as "the worst weekend in the history of the world", an asteroid or comet, five miles across and weighing a billion tons, crashed into the earth somewhere near Yucatan at twenty-five miles a second. At this speed, the atmosphere turned into flame, and when it had burned, into nitric acid. Colossal seismic waves would have drowned continents, and the temperature dropped so low that the Earth's forests freeze-dried and then burst into flames. The nitric acid from the atmosphere would have dissolved rock to pour cadmium, lead, and mercury into the water supplies. The dinosaurs were incinerated, gassed, frozen, poisoned and drowned. And Darkness lay upon the face of the Earth.

the craft was suddenly engulfed by a massive eruption as its liquid hydrogen fuel tank exploded. The two solid fuel booster rockets continued to fire, and peeled off, spinning crazily away from the shuttle, leaving two despairing smoke trails across the cloudless sky, like dying fireworks. Thousands of pieces of wreckage fell into the Atlantic. It was not until 6 March that the capsule, containing the remains of the astronauts, was recovered by divers. The nation that watched was traumatized by the public loss of life and the humiliation; they had been fed a myth of infallibility and could not believe their eyes. It produced a major loss of public confidence.

The shuttle programme was immediately suspended. In June, a President's commission on the disaster pinpointed a fault on one of the solid-fuel booster rocket seals. It had malfunctioned and sprayed the hydrogen tank with fuel, setting off the explosion. America's space programme was grounded for thirty-two months. It was 1988 before a shuttle flew again, after re-design and re-evaluation of the project. In May 1992, the shuttle undertook its first commercial repair commission, NASA having been paid $93 million to restore the orbit of an old satellite to be used to transmit the Olympic games worldwide. After three attempts, the astronauts succeeded. But the time consumed by the commercial operation left no time for any of the scientific work planned. Many still question the fundamental ethics of the shuttle; is space to be another conquest for big business and the military while that great aspiration, planetary exploration of the final frontier, is forgotten? They think that if business rules, Challenger will not be the last catastrophe, and the people involved will be dying for no greater cause than money.

Chapter Six

Apocalypse Now

T he greatest catastrophe of all goes on around us continuously, and largely unnoticed. So far reaching are its effects
that few can truly grasp the significance of the accelerating
destruction of the environment. Pollution, deforestation, over-
consumption; if all the world's food were produced by the
methods used in the USA, the total known petroleum resources
of the entire globe would be exhausted within thirteen years. By
the time you've read this page, another species will have become
extinct. Man will not necessarily be the last to go. We've known
about the problems for decades, and yet have done virtually
nothing, so unwilling have we become to change our life-styles.
There are a mere ten years left in which to save the planet's
environment. It is only the dramatic incidents of ghastly mass
pollution and poisoning that bring home to us the very real horror
that could be only years away for all; already, whether are aware
of it or not, one fifth of all people on this planet are being
murdered by the air they breathe.

The Horror of Bhopal

T he Union Carbide Corporation, manufacturer of the
EverReady battery, is one of the largest companies in
the United States. It is a multi-national, and has factories
worldwide. In common with many other huge Western
manufacturers, a good proportion of its works are located in
Third World countries. These, eager for investment, can
offer dirt-cheap labour and tend to be less stringent about

Catastrophes

> Only ten per cent of all chemicals in use have been tested fully for toxicity; information on the toxicity of eighty per cent of commercial chemicals is not available to the public.

environmental controls. Hence, some of the most toxic substances are manufactured there. When it became established in India, Union Carbide ran an advertisement which read:

'Oxen working in the fields ... the eternal river Ganges ... jewelled elephants on parade. Today these symbols of ancient India exist side by side with a new sight — modern industry ... UNION CARBIDE ...' A hand in things to come.

The Union Carbide plant at Bhopal in southern India manufactured pesticides, though frankly, the thousands living adjacent to the plant, or even working in it, had little idea what purpose the chemicals used there served. A principle ingredient in the process was methyl isocyanate, which is partly derived from phosgene, the gas used in the trenches in World War I. Safety instructions to the workers consisted principally of the instruction that, in the event of a leak, they were to leave the plant and run upwind. Workers and local inhabitants were not told about the potential, fatal effects of the chemicals. Even after the monstrous accident that was to occur, the Union Carbide chief medical officer telephoned the local hospital and told the staff that the chemical was merely an 'irritant', and should be washed off with water, when the company were well aware that it was a killer. Union Carbide would also bring other doctors over who claimed that people were dying because they were in the first place unhealthy, which is rather like a firing squad saying that their target died of a heart attack before the bullet reached him. Or even worse, it implies that the company had somehow done them a favour in curtailing their unhappy lives.

At 1 a.m., on 3 December 1984, a valve burst from over-pressure, the antiquated and ill-maintained safety systems failed and a forty-five tonne tank of methyl isocyanate was released into the atmosphere. It formed a cloud over the town. The sirens went off, but no-one knew what to do. True to their instructions, the workers ran upwind, only to find in front of them, a high concrete wall topped with barbed-wire and without gates.

When the effects of the gas became felt, panic broke out in Bhopal. People attempted to escape the cloud on foot, but it naturally moved much faster than they could. The old began to collapse, children lost their parents, the crowds swept back and forth in terror in the darkness, traffic crushed those who fell, and everyone choked, barely able to breath, their eyes red and stinging, noses steaming, convulsively vomiting; then, blindness followed.

At least 3,000 died almost immediately; some estimates make it as high as 10,000. Population figures are hard to gauge in India. What is certain is that the Indian Hindi were compelled to use mass burial, in complete breach of their faith, so great was the slaughter. Another 500,000 suffered visible after effects; blindness, permanent ill-health, disfigurement. Three people a week still die as a consequence of the leak. The town looked exactly as one would expect the target of a gas attack; corpses of cattle and children in the streets, wrecked cars and scattered possessions, the sounds of mourning, and the open doors of empty houses. Packs of dogs dug up the fresh graves.

Union Carbide denied negligence on their part. They claimed it was sabotage, and produced a leaflet demonstrating how this might have been done. In a statement to

Catastrophes

During the Vietnam War, the Americans used ecological warfare against the North Vietnamese in order to destroy the forest which provided them with cover. They used three principle herbicides, 2,4-D and 2,4,5-D, mixed with another called picloram. More than ten per cent of the country was sprayed with this potent cocktail; ten times the amounts stipulated for domestic use were employed. It killed a whole lot more than was intended. Long term, potentially irreparable damage has been done to forests, swamps and topsoil. What is now emerging are the toxic effects on both animals and man, including widespread abnormalities at birth. Information about the full effects of de-foliants used in the war are still suppressed. In 1984, a group of Vietnam Veterans won $180 million compensation from seven US chemical companies, the manufacturers of 'Agent Orange', claiming that they had been exposed to herbicides and suffered cancer, nerve, skin and liver damage. The companies settled out of court and publicly continued to deny responsibility.

investors in June 1985 they said, 'UCC does not believe that it will be or should be liable for the disastrous events at Bhopal.' There was no evidence. Everything pointed to the accident being the inevitable consequence of cost-cutting, inefficiency and the pursuit of money at the expense of human considerations. For two years, union officials at the plant had complained about safety standards. UCC por-trayed itself as a victim of Indian government interference in its management of the plant. The Indian government launched a £1,800 million lawsuit against the company for compensation on behalf of the victims. An interim payment of £150 million was made. Union Carbide will string out the legal wrangle for years; by the time it is settled, the victims will be dead. Let us hope that the Union Carbide advert is untrue; that they do not have 'a hand in things to come'.

Seveso - the Town that Died

Zone A is the dead, sealed heart of Seveso, a small Italian town north of the industrial centre of Milan. In the Sixties and early Seventies it was a popular stopping point for drivers. Ahead of them, as they came up the motorway, was the inspirational sight of the mountains above Lake Como; blue skies and the sun shining off sharp, snow-capped peaks. Behind them was the smog of Milan. Seveso was a good place to pause for fuel before journeying on into the mountains, or Switzerland. Many would spend a few hours looking round the pretty, affluent town known for its furniture. It was less well known for the Icsema chemical plant just outside the town, manufacturing a wide range of herbicides.

On 10 July 1976, there was an explosion at the Icsema plant, and a cloud of dust rose into the air and spread over the town. Officials of the plant and its owners, Hoffman La Roche, were uncertain as to the cherhical composition of the cloud and its effects. No immediate panic ensued; no dire warnings were given. Within twenty-four hours, peculiar and frightening things were happening downwind of the factory. Trees and plants died. Children developed rashes and sores and displayed sickness and high temperatures. Birds and pets began to die. It was only some days later that scientists realized what had been produced in the explosion: dioxin. By chance, the explosion had formed the released chemicals into a version of the Vietnam defoliant 'Agent Orange'.

By the time this was realized and the Seveso area declared a disaster zone, hundreds were already lying in hospital, their skin erupting horribly. Victims suffered from chloracne, a persistent eruption of weeping boils all over the body. Exposed areas, like the face had to be swathed in gauze masks and bandages. Many were burned and pock-marked for life. Children were particularly vulnerable, enduring repeated attacks over the following months. De-contamination workers wearing protective clothing contracted liver disease. Ten thousand people left town, and forty thousand pets and farm animals were dead from poisoning or had to be slaughtered. As so many inhabitants fled, the full extent of the abnormalities in births caused by the chemical catastrophe remains unknown. Cancer is another long-term consequence. But, as in Vietnam, the true effects take years to emerge, and are shrouded in secrecy and denial. No-one can say how far the shadow of the cloud extended. Four months after the tragedy, traces of dioxin were found in soil in the centre of Milan.

Years later, tests revealed that soil outside the main area of contamination in Seveso still contained levels of poison ten times greater than was predicted. The centre of the disaster was also the centre of town. This was designated Zone A by the authorities and will remained sealed off for ever. Dioxin, the most insidious poison known to man, never dies. In Zone A, the topsoil from other less con-taminated areas was dumped and buildings were demol-ished. Around Zone A, a fence, ten foot high was erected. Entry is by special government permission only. Those who left their houses have never returned. Astonishingly, looters have run the insane risk of stripping the wreckage of anything of value.

On the approach to the town, someone painted a skull and cross-bones on the sign carrying its name. Nobody stops there anymore, not even a passing bird. Hoffman La Roche paid £57 million in compensation, but claimed it was a freak chance that led to the disaster. It was apparent that little thought had been paid to the possible consequences of a fire or explosion, and little was truly known about the long term effects of toxic substances produced and used everywhere. They call Seveso, 'Italy's Hiroshima'.

The London Smog

Poor air quality is part of everyday city life now; an unwelcome addition to the weather forecast. Modem Western cities tend to be smoke-free zones, within which the burning of coal is forbidden, hence the smog is 'photochemical', caused by the effect of the suns rays on traffic fumes, and just because you can't see it doesn't mean it isn't there. You can smell the sulphur. Sometimes, extraordinary weather conditions mean that heavy freezing fog mingles with car and industrial fumes to form a grey, acidic shroud over cities. Nothing is now quite so obviously poisonous as the London "Pea Soupers" of 1952.

In the wake of an influenza epidemic, dreadful weather and coastal flooding, came a thick blanket of pollution-based fog that reduced visibility to few feet, invaded the lungs with bitter, choking poison and bought chaos to the city. Within a fortnight, 4,000 people had been killed by the dense sulphur dioxide fumes, which reached a level of 1.3 parts per million, far higher than the level legal inside a factory producing the poison, let alone residential areas. It had a particularly vicious effect on the lungs of the old and the young.

Freak weather failed to bring any wind strong enough to disperse it; instead, the icy winds chilled it and spread the

Catastrophes

in 1956, a revolutionary new drug was placed on the market. Thalidomide, doctors were told, was a major advance in the field of sedatives. Unlike other drugs used to induce sleep, Thalidomide was not potentially fatal if an overdose was taken. It could be used on young children with complete safety, and could be bought without prescription. Five years later, in 1961, doctors across the world became concerned about the number of deformed children being born. Most of these children lacked arms or legs. It was found that the mothers all had one thing in common; they had taken a sedative containing Thalidomide during pregnancy. An article by a German doctor called Lenz, in a medical publication, made the connection public, and most, but not all drugs containing Thalidomide were withdrawn. Some continued to be sold, and, unaware of the danger, people continued to use the drugs they had already purchased. By the time proper investigation had been conducted into the side-effects of the drug, there were two hundred and seventy-five deformed children in Britain and 5,000 in Germany. Another 5,000 died at birth or in early childhood. More died later. Those who survived are now in their late-twenties, and still living with their drug induced deformities: it took them years to win compensation.

sulphur dioxide further. The smog, largely due to domestic coal smoke, plunged London back into a Victorian world of

It's true, man-made killer bees are on the loose. In 1956, scientists in Brazil imported African queen bees to cross breed with European varieties in order to produce a more productive bee. A year later, twenty-six swarms escaped and began their inexorable progression northwards. They cross-breed easily with other strains and the hybrid swarms spread very fast. The bees are large and distinguished by their sheer ferocity. They will launch massive, unprovoked attacks on any living thing in their path. Their sting is fatal to animals and men. They move continuously and their huge swarms have already reached the Southern States of the USA, which means they have travelled 6,834 miles. Perhaps the colder weather of the north will bring them to a halt.

coughing pedestrians, stumbling through streets where the lights from traffic and houses were reduced to faint glowing halos and where the only people enjoying themselves were criminals, who reduced large sections of the population to a state of abject terror. Apart from the victims of crime, many died in traffic related accidents; it was an unknown world outside. As one man recalled:

"There were some days during that fortnight when you couldn't see your own hand stuck out in front of you. At times, the streets were deserted, save for the villains, who made rich pickings. It seemed like the entire city was one giant morgue. If you wanted to remain safe you stayed indoors ... to venture out on the roads was suicidal, you could cut the air with a knife. The stench of sulphur was unbelievable; every breath you took left you gasping or threw you into a convulsive fit of coughing."

As a result, Parliament voted to set up an emergency Atmospheric Pollution committee, and the burning of coal was banned within London, but smog cause by traffic fumes is becoming more frequent and more visible. Other Western cities have already banned cars from their centres. It is only a matter of time before London is obliged to.

The Torrey Canyon and the Amoco Cadiz

The wreck of the oil tanker Torrey Canyon off the coast of Britain in March 1967 began a new chapter in history; that of catastrophic oil slicks. Before the Torrey Canyon ripped itself open on the Seven Stones reef near Land's End, there was little public awareness of the consequences of oil pollution. When, within hours, 30,000 tonnes of crude oil started to come ashore on the beaches of Cornwall there was no escaping the effects, but little knowledge of what to do. Twenty-five thousand sea-birds were killed. Detergent was poured into the sea and along the beaches which are some of the oldest and most beautiful on England's coastline; the thick layer of black sand was scraped away, and even flamethrowers were used. So inexperienced in this kind of disaster were the emergency teams that the work was patchy and haphazard. The detergents used were as poisonous as the oil, and marine life suffered terribly from both. The RAF bombed the wreck in order to try and burn the oil remaining inside, but by that time, a storm had broken up the ship and another 3,000 tonnes were floating towards the coast. In all, 110,000 tonnes spewed out of the tanker.

The Torrey Canyon oil tanker, after being split in two on the Seven Stones rocks off Land's end.

The oil reached the Channel Islands and France, where they attempted in vain to sink it with vast quantities of sawdust. Oil was still being washed ashore in the Bay of Biscay three months later. As the areas affected were all dependent on fishing and tourism, the disaster of pollution was followed by financial ruin for many. The public had lost its innocence about oil pollution.

It was only the first of a long string of ever-escalating disasters. In March 1978, nine years later, the Amoco Cadiz, a tanker carrying 220,000 tonnes of crude oil ran aground near the fishing village of Portsall in Brittany, France ... The initial cause was a fault in the steering mechanism, but the captain was also accused of failing to act quickly enough to save his ship; it was alleged that while it crashed into the rocks, he was busy arguing with a tug-boat captain about the price of being towed to safety. It was not until twelve

The wrecked Torrey Canyon oil tanker, after being bombed by forty-six RAF and Navy jets in a plan to burn off its remaining cargo of oil.

hours after the tanker had first run into trouble that distress rockets were sent up to alert the authorities; by that time the ship was already holed. The conduct of the captains in both tanker and tug was disgraceful. The tug responded to a radio message from the tanker requesting assistance. After having linked the two ships with a line, the two settled down to lengthy negotiations in a cabin. The Italian captain of the Amoco Cadiz insisted that his ship was in no real danger; this was not a salvage operation, and all he needed was a tow back to an English port for brief repairs, The tug captain, a German, wanted to claim it as a 'Lloyd's open contract', a salvage operation which would require the owners of the Amoco Cadiz to pay a percentage of the $20 million value of the ship's cargo. Whilst they wrangled, the French authorities worried by the drift of the Amoco Cadiz, repeatedly radioed to check that things were in hand, and were consistently told that everything was fine. By the time the two captains had reached an agreement - that the tug owner would get his percentage - the weather had deteriorated, the line between the two ships snapped, and the huge bulk of the Amoco Cadiz ran into the rocks.

Oil is carried on board a tanker within a series of separate tanks; in the case of some wrecks, not all of these are ruptured. On the Amoco Cadiz, they were; the total cargo poured into the sea. A brisk wind helped to extend the slick along several hundred miles of the French coast. The French responded by using inflatable booms to try and drive the oil off the coast, but the weather was bad and wind and waves made them useless. Experience had by now taught that detergents were an equal evil, so they could do nothing but watch the black tide pour ashore. The oil was a thin variety which meant that it penetrated the sand to a depth of nineteen inches, and could not be scraped away. It was there to stay. That area is also dependent on fishing and tourism, and was also devastated, though the sea demonstrates an uncanny capacity to cleanse, and most visible signs of the

The shipwrecked supertanker Amoco Cadiz after being torn apart by rough seas.

The Amoco Cadiz on her way down.

disaster were eventually washed away. It is the invisible, but murderous, long-term effect of oil pollution on marine life, and by implication, our own food supplies that is as yet, only partially understood.

Catastrophes

Aberfan is the name of a small, secluded Welsh mining village, a respectable and tight-knit community that was destroyed at 9.15 a.m. on 21 October, 1966. Looming above the village was the spectre of Pantglas Coaltip no. 7, a huge mountain of slag some eight hundred feet high, that many residents had feared posed a threat to the village, and dreaded the day when it might move. Their complaints about safety had been ignored. That morning, made mobile by rain, the tower of rubbish began to move, just at the time when infants in the Pantglas Junior School were attending a morning service on the final morning before their half-term holiday. The waste slipped rapidly down on the village and engulfed the school and nineteen other houses, travelling over half a mile before it finally stopped. Five teachers, twenty-three other adults and one hundred and sixteen children between the ages of seven and ten were killed. There was not a family in the village that was not affected. In the aftermath, the heartless glare of publicity and the generosity of the relief funds both left the community confused, saddened and embittered; even those who had survived felt guilty for escaping. A whole generation had vanished; and like so many tragedies, it need never have happened.

Chapter Seven

Bridge Disasters

I t's easy to get a phobia about bridges. They can look magnificent without ever giving one the slightest confidence in their absolute safety.

Safe Crossing?

O n Christmas Eve 1953, most people in New Zealand were either already in the midst of family gatherings or were hurrying back home to join in the celebrations. On New Zealand's North Island, an active volcano, Mount Ruahepu, stirred vaguely. It was not a massive eruption, but it set off a catastrophic sequence of events. The volcano has a crater lake, full of sulphurous water that heats up when the volcano becomes active. Since the volcano had last erupted in 1948, the outlet from the lake had become blocked with debris and ice; as a result the lake had become dangerously overfull.

On 28 December 1879, the Tay Bridge in Scotland collapsed in terrible storms. The 5.20 from Burntisland to Dundee arrived to find there was no bridge. It could not stop, and plunged ninety foot into the raging waters of the Tay, where all seventy-five on board drowned.

Catastrophes

In Sydney, Australia, on 18 January 1977, a rush hour express train took a corner too fast and came off the rails, knocking away the supports from an over-hanging road bridge, which pancaked on top of the train, reducing some carriages to a metre in height. They had to use cranes to lift the bridge sections off the train in which eighty had died.

Ships not infrequently crash into bridges. In 1980, this happened twice within months, when two Liberian-registered ships destroyed the supports on road bridges, one in Sweden near Gothenburg and one in Tampa Bay, Florida. In the first, fifteen people died after cars plunged thirty-seven metres into icy water. In the second, the cargo ship removed a 400-metre section of a four lane highway on the fourteen mile span of the Sunshine Skyway Bridge. A bus, two cars and a lorry fell into the turbulent waters. Other cars screeched to a halt at the very edge of the chasm. Thirty people died.

When the volcano stirred on Christmas Eve, it was just sufficient to breach the barrier and send nearly three billion litres of scalding, acidic water and associated mud and rubbish cascading into the Whangaehu River. The Placid river became a torrent and swept downstream, threatening roads and weakening bridges. The Wellington Express, a train carrying holiday travellers to Auckland, approached its bridge across the river in complete ignorance of what was happening. In vain, a young postal worker called Ellis ran along the track and tried to warn the Express by waving his torch. The train could not stop. The moment it rolled onto the bridge, it collapsed, and the engine and its first five coaches dived into the murderous river. The sixth coach teetered on the edge of the precipice and then also fell. One hundred and fifty-one people died in this accident at the most unfortunate time of year.

A popular, cheap and fast way of building bridges seemed for a number of years to be the box-girder method, using vast pre-fabricated steel boxes, which can then be slotted in next to each other. It did not allow for much adaptation to individual circumstances, and a series of catastrophes falling in quick succession of each other, put paid to its credibility. First, a bridge under construction across the Danube collapsed in 1969.

A year later, a bridge fell and killed several workmen at Milford Haven in Wales. Only months later, an enormous bridge also under construction, across the Yarra River in Australia buckled and collapsed, shedding eighty tons of concrete onto workmen below, of whom thirty-five were killed. It seems that two of the box-sections had failed to meet by as little as half an inch; in their efforts to correct this, engineers had put too much stress on an already weak structure.

Chapter Eight

The Runaway Train

T rains are generally considered to be one of the safest means
of transport, except under overcrowded conditions. However, the modern dependence on technology places enormous faith
in equipment which is not infallible. Each year, there are fewer
staff on trains, fewer staff operating the rail networks, more
technology. People can fail just as badly as machinery; sometimes
their behaviour is not explicable.

The Moorgate Tragedy

L.B. Newson was the regular motorman on the Highbury
branch of the London Underground Northern Line, shut-
tling a train up and down a two-and-three-quarter mile
stretch of track, a seven minute journey, from Drayton Park
to Moorgate and back, Moorgate being one of the principal
stations in the business centre of London's City. Newson
was a fifty-six-year-old man, who had only been working on
the railways for six years, and had only made thirty-seven
trips before he was made a motorman in January 1975, a
little more than a month before the accident in which he was
to play such a crucial and inexplicable role. All those who
knew him said that they had not noticed anything strained
or unusual about him in the days prior to the catastrophe,
and he was under no strain from work, having done a usual
week's shift, with no overtime and a day off.

At 8.06 a.m. on the 28 February, Newson drove a train
full of rush hour commuters into the Moorgate terminus at

In the early morning of 8 October 1952, three trains - a slow commuter train headed for London, the Perth Express heading for Scotland, and the 7.55 Express from Euston to Liverpool and Manchester - were involved in an horrendous collision at Harrow Station. The pile of wreckage was the worst ever seen in Britain. It was fortunate that there were few passengers on board otherwise the death toll of one hundred and twelve would have been much higher. The Perth Express had ignored the signals at Harrow. As the driver and fireman were dead, no reason could be found for their conduct.

full speed, without making any attempt to apply the brakes and crashed it violently into the end of a short extension tunnel beyond the station platform. Those who watched him drive through the station at its unchecked speed said he appeared absolutely calm.

So mangled was the wreckage, it was thirteen hours and nineteen minutes until the last body - that of Newson was freed. He, and forty-two passengers were dead, and seventy-four were injured. The inquiry found no mechanical failure whatsoever; they could only conclude that Newson had decided to do this deliberately.

As a general point, they realized that there was no system to cope with the eventuality of a suicidal driver, and installed one on the Underground. Now, if a driver deliberately overruns a stop signal indicating danger, the brakes are automatically applied. On the British Railways system there is an electronic emergency signalling device, which will also apply the brakes but only if the driver does

not acknowledge it. As it tends to be impossible to prove
suicidal intent on the part of the driver, the risk is
considered too small to make an issue out of.

The Lost Battalion

On 22 May, 1915, Britain was involved in the most awful
war the world had ever known. Whilst the civilian population went about their lives and tried to keep a semblance of
normality, all around, the young were departing for the
killing fields of Flanders. Early that morning, at the Scottish
railway station of Larbet, five hundred men and officers of
the 1/7th Battalion of the Royal Scots climbed on board a
twenty-one vehicle troop train to start their long journey.
On its way to its confidential destination, the train would
pass through Quintinshill, a small signals points, where
additional loops on the track provided space for berthing
freight trains off the busy line. From Quintinshill, about ten
miles outside Carlisle, the track running north into Scotland
had a long, steady upward gradient of about 1:200. Trains
running down from Scotland, as the troop 'Special' would
be, picked up a lot of speed.

The consequences of what happened that day are grim;
but the series of events that conspired to bring the accident
about are fascinating. It is an almost inevitable chain of
consequence.

Late the previous night, two trains had left Euston in
London, headed for Scotland, one at 11.45 p.m. for
Edinburgh, and one at midnight, for Glasgow. They should
have left Carlisle and made for these destinations at 5.50
a.m. and 6.05 a.m. respectively. At 6.10 a.m., a third train
was due to leave Carlisle and follow them up the same line.
This was the all-stations, slow local, known as the 'Parley',
which picked up passengers from the tiny, roadside stations,

and took them on to Beattock. It had a connection to make at 7.49 at Beattock, and the company running the line, the Caledonian Railway, took great pride in the punctuality of its trains.

The London and North Western Railway, which ran the two night-time trains from Euston, also set great store by its ability to keep to schedule. However, these two night-time trains were always bad time-keepers, and were consistently up to half an hour late at Carlisle. In order not to delay the 6.10 'Parley', the Caledonian Railway would send it off if the fast trains were more than fifteen to twenty minutes late, and then move it onto a side track further down the line in order to clear the way for the two fast trains, which by that time had normally left Carlisle and were steaming up behind it. When they had passed, it would be shunted back onto the main track, and continue to chug its way up to Beattock. In the six months prior to the 22nd of May, the 6.10 'Parley' had been shunted out of the way twenty-one times at Quintinshill. Here the freight berths provided plenty of space for it.

The fact that the train frequently stopped at this remote signals box suited the two signalmen, Tinsley and Meakin, who worked alternate shifts. The journey from Gretna, where they both lived, to the box, was about one and a half miles on foot or bicycle. Before setting off, they would ask the signalman at Gretna if the 'Parley' was due to be shunted out of the way at Quintinshill; if he said yes, they would wait at Gretna for the 'Parley', and ride on the footplate to Quintinshill. Innocent though this seems, it led them into a breach of regulations, the consequences of which would contribute to the catastrophe.

They ought to have been swapping over at 6 a.m. If the 'Parley' was due to stop at Quintinshill, the night man would cease to make direct entries in the train register at that time, and write them down on a separate piece of paper. Then, when the day man arrived later, on the 'Parley', he would copy these entries into the train register in his own hand, so that any official checking the register would not be able to tell from the hand-writing that the change of shifts had not taken place at the authorized time of 6 a.m.

On the morning of the 22nd, the night express trains were running half an hour late. The 6.10 'Parley' left Carlisle ahead of them. At Gretna, Tinsley, who was due to work the day shift, hopped on the footplate and rode up to Quintinshill where the 'Parley' was yet again to be side-tracked. There, he discovered a problem. The side-loop of track he would normally shunt the 'Parley' into was occupied by a goods train. He would have to side-track the 'Parley' by crossing it over and placing it on the main, south-bound track. This dangerous sounding manoeuvre was quite safe, provided the safety precautions were followed to the letter; the next signal box north at Kirkpatrick had to know there was a train blocking the south-bound line. They had done this four times in the last sixth months.

The first night express passed safely northwards at 6.38 a.m. Meanwhile, on the south-bound track, where the 'Parley' was still sitting, waiting for the second express to pass, things became more confused. A train load of empty coal wagons arrived, and were put in the south-bound siding. In the signals box, Tinsley was preoccupied copying in the entries which Meakin, the night man, had made on a sheet of paper prior to his arrival. Meakin had not gone off immediately, but was reading Tinsley's newspaper. While Tinsley copied, the two men chattered about the war. Tinsley was not concentrating. At some point, one of the men (though both denied it) sent a message to the signal man at Kirkpatrick indicating that the coal wagons were off the south-bound track; *they omitted to say that the 'Parley' was still on it.*

In addition, neither man ensured that the signal levers for the south-bound line had protective collars on them to ensure that the line could not be used. Even the fireman from the 'Parley', who had popped up to the box failed to notice this. The scene was set for a cataclysm.

At 6.42 a.m. the Kirkpatrick box, which presumed that the south-bound track must be clear, 'offered' the troop train to Quintinshill. Distracted by his copying, still talking to Meakin, and without looking out the window to where the 'Parley' was sitting, Tinsley pulled all the signal levers for the south-bound track, indicating the line was clear. Moments later, the other delayed night-time express was also 'offered' to Quintinshill. Again, Tinsley accepted it and pulled all his signals on the north-bound track.

Towards this fated little point on the map were rushing two trains. Northwards came the night express travelling at 70 mph. Southwards, gathering momentum down the 1:200 gradient came the troop train also doing 70 mph. On the south-bound track, with its brakes locked on, sat the four carriages and engine of the 'Parley', the local train.

The troop train came sweeping down the gradient and through the curve into Quintinshill, where it collided head on at full speed with the standing 'Parley'.

The troop train, which measured two hundred and thirty-seven yards, was instantly compressed by the force of the collision to a mere sixty-seven yards. Both trains were then buried under a heap of shattered coaches from the troop train, many of which were flung clean over the engine. Portions of both the troop train and the 'Parley' were now strewn across the north-bound line, as the night express to Glasgow finally came steaming up the track, with another twenty-two carriages drawn by two engines. It ploughed into the wreckage at 60mph and hit the tender from the 'Parley', which was lying directly across the track. The express came violently to a halt, its coaches telescoping.

With burning coals scattered from the wrecked engines among the landscape of wrecked wooden coaches, a fire broke out, which raged for twenty-four hours. Those who had not died in the crash were now burned to death; it was impossible to rescue them.

The true death toll for the Scots Guards is not known, as the Battalion Roll and records were lost in the fire. The survivors paraded in a field next to the wreck. Out of the five hundred who boarded the train, only fifty-two were left.

The official casualty figures for the troops were given as two hundred and fifteen dead, and one hundred and ninety-one injured, though it was thought that these figures were kept low for 'reasons of public morale' during a time of war.

Surprisingly, there were only ten civilians killed and fifty-one injured. As for the unlucky Tinsley and Meakin, they were convicted of manslaughter and received long sentences.

The "Black Market Express"

In March 1944, World War II was about to enter its final stage. In three months, Allied forces would land in France. They were already in Italy, and had liberated much of the country from the Germans. In the midst of war, the economy was in ruins; the normal means of trade and barter were not possible. The Black Market, although officially illegal, was unofficially accepted as a part of life, one of the few ways that often essential foodstuffs could reach the poor, deprived cities of southern Italy.

There was a regular train running weekly out of Salerno to Potenza, which was customarily packed to the gills with illegal passengers from Salerno and the neighbouring city of Naples, going to the country to trade on the Black Market. They would take with them cigarettes and chocolate obtained from the occupying forces of the Allies and exchange these luxury items for meat, oil, eggs and wine

One of the worst commuter catastrophes
happened about three miles north of Tokyo in
May 1963. A commuter train was hit by a steam-
driven freight train. A third train, coming from
behind, then piled into the derailed coaches. On
the commuter train, special doors which opened
in the event of an emergency only worsened the
nightmare; they came open as planned, and
passengers were flung over a thirty-foot
embankment. There were one hundred and
sixty-three casualties.

in the prosperous farming town of Potenza. On 2 March,
1944, the train, No. 8017 pulling forty-two carriages, set off
from Salerno. At the stations along its route, or even where
it slowed down, passengers piled on board with their caches
of contraband. At early stops the Military Police would
make a token effort to kick off illegal passengers, but more
would take their place. By the time the train approached the
Apennine Mountain range where it would have to cross on
the final stretch to Potenza, it was dragging. At Romagua-
no, they added another engine to help it up the steep
gradient. The driver and firemen cursed the coal that they
were stoking the engines with; it was inferior brown coal,
which burned badly, smoked too much and produced little
heat. But it was war-time, and they had no option. They just
had to use more of it.

Shortly before midnight, the train stopped at Balvano, a
mountain village. It was forced to stop, as there was another
train ahead with problems. It was a cold night, the rails icy
and slippery. The Black Market Express sat, quietly puffing
smoke. Balvano is situated in between two tunnels. So long
was the train, that half of it remained hidden in the tunnel to

Catastrophes

At Christmas 1915, in the midst of World War I, an overloaded French troop train carrying 1,200 soldiers back from the Front for Christmas derailed coming down a steep gradient. The carriages fell into a gorge and burst into flames. Officially, five hundred and forty-three died, but it was privately acknowledged that the true total had been suppressed for reasons of public morale. The driver had objected to the obvious overloading, but was threatened with a court-martial and execution if he failed to obey orders.

its rear for the hour long duration it was stationary. The poor quality coal belched smoke, which drifted back over the carriages. It was an unpleasant hour for many of the passengers. Some were surprised at how drowsy they felt in spite of the acute cold.

Leaving Balvano at last, the train began a steep climb. Ahead of it lay another tunnel, the Galleria del Armi, over two miles long, and on a very sharp uphill gradient. When the train entered it, and was completely engulfed, the firemen and driver began to have problems. The ice on the tracks was causing the wheels to slip, in spite of the additional engine. No-one really knew how many people were on board or the weight of their luggage, but it was proving to be too much. But the real problem was the damn coal; they just could not get up a decent head of steam with it. They began to stoke the fire furiously.

At the far rear of the train was the brakeman. His truck was only just inside the tunnel. He could still see the night and the stars, and breathe the mountain air, though he admitted that the smoke from the engine was quite disgusting. For some minutes the train had been completely stationary, the wheels still and with no sign of movement from the front. Indeed, the whole train seemed remarkably silent. He decided to take a look.

Hopping out of his truck, he took a lantern and strolled up the side of the train.

On his way, he peered through the windows of the first passenger carriage. Inside it was dark and utterly silent, and everybody was quite clearly dead. With growing terror, he ran along the side of the train; in every carriage it was the same. People sat and leant comfortably, as if sleeping, bent over, their faces curiously rosy, no signs of violence, or resistance. And there were the train's crew, slumped peacefully on the floor of the leading engine. They had all been gassed by carbon monoxide from the cheap coal. Wailing, the brakeman turned and started to run down the hill to Balvano.

The Allied Court of Inquiry concluded that this must be the most remarkable train catastrophe ever, as it involved no collision or derailment, and there was nothing technically wrong with the train. It was the coal, which produced an uncommonly high proportion of carbon monoxide, which, they guessed must have killed most of the occupants of the train within minutes of entering the tunnel. There were five hundred and twenty-one dead, and only five survivors, all of whom suffered the lasting side effects, including madness, that oxygen deprivation brings to the brain. Many of the bodies remained unclaimed by their families and were never identified. They were buried in a mass grave. They say that the tunnel remains haunted by the ghosts of the Black Market Express.

America's First Rail Catastrophes

Many of the early disasters on the American railways became the subject of popular ballads with titles like 'The

Catastrophes

Chatsworth Wreck'. This particular ditty commemorated a train that drove onto a bridge that was on fire, killing eighty-two. Another highly popular ballad was 'The Wreck of Old '97', which was renowned among the mountain people of Virginia and North Carolina. American folklore has a sneaking fondness for the memory of all drivers whose vehicles were destroyed because they were going too fast. In train mythology, their enduring celebrity is best represented by the fame of John Latimer 'Casey' Jones, engineer of the Illinois Central First Mail Train No.1, known as 'The Cannonball'. Quite without reason, he ploughed at full speed into another train in Mississipi on 30 April 1900. Casey was the only one to die, which is perhaps why he is remembered affectionately.

Chapter Nine

All at Sea

C atastrophes at sea are the stuff of myth and legend, and the origin of some of the greatest stories of true heroism. Since the demise of the ocean liner as a means of mass transport, there have been fewer major disasters involving great loss of human life; the aircraft has taken over. But some of the worst incidents have occurred where they can never be seen.

They Never Surfaced

S ubmarines have been in use for longer than most people think. Since the first one sailed in 1774, nearly 2,000 have been lost. In World War II, Germany alone lost seven hundred and eighty-seven submarines excluding those that were scuttled on its surrender. During war, submarines are particularly liable to be bombed by their own side. Even in peace, submarining is highly hazardous; the deep oceans remain the last unexplored, and often uncharted areas in the world. Due to the military nature of their operations, details surrounding accidents are often carefully guarded. Few survive; the underwater killers are also coffins.

The most dramatic peacetime submarine disaster known of is undoubtedly that involving the USS 'Thresher', an American submarine which met a shadowy end in 1963. It was a highly significant incident, because the USS 'Thresher' was the world's first nuclear power submarine to be lost.

Catastrophes

Thresher had always suffered from apparently minor, but potentially serious problems. During her first year of service, the air conditioning system had failed more than once, raising the internal temperature to a lethal 136°F. Its blowing system which expelled the water had also been incorrectly wired. There was a distinct possibility of it flooding under certain circumstances. Other problems cropped up, and after a year of service, it went back to the Naval Yard for refitting and modification, an overhaul which took 100,000 man-hours. Even after this, problems continued; its water suction valves refused to close, its torpedo tube shutters malfunctioned. More work was done on it, but the crew were heard to mutter that they felt the re-fitting had been too rushed.

Thresher left Portsmouth Naval Base in America on 9 April, accompanied by the rescue ship 'Skylark'. It was due to carry out deep-sea trials about two hundred and twenty miles off Boston, in the Gulf of Maine. At 7.47 a.m., Thresher commenced a deep-dive, conducting checks and manoeuvres. Down went the submarine, towards its secret test-depth. All the time it kept in contact with Skylark, whose Captain became concerned that the voice contact with Thresher was oddly distorted, as if coming from a long, long way off. The submarine was well below four hundred feet, when the Skylark's captain received the last message from the Thresher; ". . . have positive up angle. Attempting. . ." At the same time, the captain heard the Thresher close its vents and blow compressed air into the ballast tanks, as if attempting to rise. Then, nothing else. Or, nothing else that the Military would explain to the public. There was one more signal logged; it went simply '900N'. The Navy refused to say what this meant; it might indicate that the submarine was more than nine hundred feet under water, below its test-depth. There was also one noise recorded; a dull, muted groan, as the submarine broke up.

A massive search was launched by the US Government; not only to try and find out what happened, but because they were concerned that the nuclear power unit would leak from any wreck. They used every conceivable scientific instrument; underwater TV cameras, echo-sounders, geiger counters and a bathyscaphe. It was this last device that eventually found the Thresher - or what remained of it. It was lying on the ocean bottom at a depth of 8,400 feet. Details of what was seen have never been given, but it seems that the top-secret submarine had been crushed by the water pressure of 3,700 pounds per square inch, and was scattered in thousands of pieces over a huge area. There was also a large crater in the sea bed, where much of the submarine may still be. The reasons why the Thresher disintegrated were never revealed. It goes without saying that no trace of the crew of one hundred and twenty-nine was ever found.

Submarines can disappear so completely that their fate remains a mystery even to the military authorities. 1968 was a vintage year for disappearances: on 25 January, an Israeli submarine vanished in the Mediterranean with her entire crew of sixty-nine. Two days later, also in the Mediterranean, a French submarine also vanished with fifty-two crew. No trace of either was ever found. In May of the same year, there was an even stranger disaster involving the USS 'Scorpion', a nuclear-powered submarine carrying sixty-nine officers and men. Returning to Norfolk Naval Base in Virginia from the Mediterranean, she last made contact with the authorities at 8 a.m. on the 21 May. She was then two hundred and fifty miles west of the Azores, and everything was entirely normal. Then the Scorpion disappeared. Five months later, she was found, four hundred and sixty miles southwest of the Azores, in 10,000 feet of water. The hull was absolutely intact; there was no explanation available as to why she had sunk or why she was so far off course. Much was written about the fact that the Scorpion had sunk on the edge of the legendary Sargasso sea, adjacent to the Bermuda Triangle, that strange area of the ocean where so many have disappeared. There was another unexplained aspect to the incident; how on earth had the Navy managed to find the Scorpion, when she was within such a vast radius of her original position, and at such a depth? And how had the hull survived intact? The Navy would not comment on either point.

Whilst the American and their Allies lost submarines during the Cold War, so did the Russians, though details of these are even harder to come by. In that same year of 1968, a Russian submarine grabbed the world headlines in a story even more bizarre than that of the Scorpion. As usual, the Americans tracked the progress of the Russian submarine from its base at Vladivostock to a point 1,000 miles northwest of Hawaii. All Russian submarines were routinely tracked by the Americans and vice-versa. It was all quite normal, until the American surveillance officers realized that the engine noises had ceased, and that the faint boom they had just heard was the sound of an explosion; a Russian submarine had blown up and sunk somewhere in the central Pacific. The Russians combed the area without success, and left. The American Navy felt that there was little on board the submarine that could be of interest to them militarily; but the White House decided that information relevant to their nuclear negotiations with the Russians could be gained by salvaging the vessel; it was carrying three nuclear ballistic missiles. The job was given the CIA, who launched "Operation Jennifer" one of the most spectacular salvage operations ever attempted, in total secrecy. It was to take years.

In 1969, they offered the billionaire business man Howard Hughes $350 million to raise the Russian submarine. He accepted, and secretly, two deep-sea salvage ships were built, under the pretence that they were for

In April 1973, a nuclear-powered Russian submarine sank only seventy miles off Land's End, Cornwall, with the loss of all eighty-eight crew, cause unknown.

deep-sea mining. They did not set out for their destination until the middle of 1974, still claiming that they were on exploratory mining missions. They found the submarine in 16,600 feet of water. What they saw was again never revealed, although it was said that seventy Russian bodies were recovered. Some American journalists say that the whole submarine, miraculously still in one piece, was retrieved by the CIA and is now in their possession. In 1968, the Russians lost yet another nuclear submarine, which sank near the Arctic Circle. When it was salvaged, they discovered that the ninety crew had survived in their icy tomb for some time; all the vessel's food stocks had been eaten.

The Bermuda Triangle, Unexplained Disasters

In the afternoon of 5 December 1945, five Avenger torpedo-bombers took off from Fort Lauderdale, Florida, for a routine two-hour patrol over the Atlantic. Flight 19 was commanded by Flight Leader Charles Taylor; the other four pilots were trainees, flying what is known as a "milk run", that is, a flight whose purpose is simply to increase their number of hours in the air without instructors. By 2.15 the planes were well over the Atlantic, and following their usual patrol route. The weather was warm and clear.

Catastrophes

At 3.45 the control tower received a message from Taylor: "This is an emergency. We seem to be off course. We cannot see land ... repeat ... we cannot see land."

"What is your position?"

"We're not sure of our position. We can't be sure where we are. We seem to be lost."

"Head due west," replied the tower.

"We don't know which way is west. Everything is wrong ... strange. We can't be sure of any direction. Even the ocean doesn't look as it should."

The tower was perplexed; even if some kind of magnetic interference caused all five compasses to malfunction, the pilot should still be able to see the sun low in the western sky. Radio contact was now getting worse, restricting any messages to short sentences. At one point the tower picked up one pilot speaking to another, saying that all the instruments in 'his plane were "going crazy". At 4 o'clock the flight leader decided to hand over to someone else. At 4.25 the new leader told the tower: "We're not certain where we are."

Unless the planes could find their way back over land during the next four hours, they would run out of fuel and be forced to land in the sea. At 6.27 a rescue mission was launched. A giant Martin Mariner flying-boat, with a crew of thirteen, took off towards the last reported position of the flight. Twenty-three minutes later, the sky to the east was lit briefly by a bright orange flash. Neither the Martin Mariner nor the five Avengers ever returned. They vanished completely, as other planes and ships have vanished in the area that has become known as "the Devil's Triangle" and "the Bermuda Triangle".

What finally happened to the missing aircraft is certainly no mystery. The weather became worse during the course of that afternoon; ships reported "high winds and tremendous seas". Flight 19 and its would-be rescuer must have run out of fuel, and landed in the sea. The mystery is *why* they became so completely lost and confused. Even if, the navigation instruments had ceased to function, and visibility had become restricted to a few yards, it should have been possible to fly up above the clouds to regain their bearings.

What seems stranger still is that this tragedy should have failed to alert the authorities that there was something frightening and dangerous about the stretch of ocean between Florida and the Bahamas - a chain of islands that begins a mere fifty miles off the coast of Florida. But then the authorities no doubt took the view of many more recent sceptics, that the disappearance was a rather complex accident, due to a number of chance factors: bad weather, electrical interference with the compasses, the inexperience of some of the pilots and the fact that the flight leader, Charles Taylor, had only recently been posted to Fort Lauderdale and was unfamiliar with the area.

Similar explanations were adopted to explain a number of similar tragedies during the next two decades: the disappearance of a Superfortress in 1947, of a four-engined Tudor IV in January 1948, of a DC3 in December 1948, of another Tudor IV in 1949, of a Globernaster in 1950, of a British York transport plane in 1952, of a Navy Super Constellation in 1954, of another Martin seaplane in 1956, of an Air Force tanker in 1962, of two Stratotankers in 1963, of a flying boxcar in 1965, of a civilian cargo plane in 1966, another cargo plane in 1967, and yet another in 1973 ... The total number of lives lost in all these disappearances was well in excess of two hundred. Oddly enough, the first person to realize that all this amounted to a frightening mystery was a journalist called Vincent Gaddis; it was in February 1964 that his article "The Deadly Bermuda Triangle" appeared in the American Argosy magazine, and bestowed the now familiar name on that mysterious stretch of ocean. A year later, in a book about sea mysteries called *Invisible Horizons*, Gaddis included his article in a chapter called "The Triangle of Death". His chapter also contained a long list of ships which had vanished in the area, beginning with the *Rosalie*, which vanished in 1840, and ending with the yacht *Connemara IV* in 1956. In the final chapter Gaddis entered the realm of science fiction, and speculated on "space-time continua [that] may exist around us on the earth, interpenetrating our known world", implying that perhaps some of the missing planes and ships had vanished down a kind of fourth-dimensional plughole.

Soon after the publication of his book Gaddis received a letter from a man called Gerald Hawkes, who told of his own experience in the Bermuda Triangle in April 1952. On a flight from Idlewild Airport (now Kennedy) to Bermuda, Hawkes's plane suddenly dropped about two hundred feet. This was not a nose-dive, but felt as if he had suddenly fallen down a lift-shaft in the air; then the plane shot back up again. "It was as if a giant hand was holding the plane and jerking it up and down," and the wings seemed to flap like the wings of a bird. The captain then told them that he was unable to find Bermuda, and that the operator was unable to make radio contact with either the US or Bermuda. An hour or so later the plane made contact with a radio ship, and was able to get its bearings and fly to Bermuda. As they climbed out of the plane they observed that it was a clear and starry night, with no wind. The writer concluded that he was still wondering whether he was caught in an area "where time and space seem to disappear".

Now, all pilots know about air pockets, where a sudden change in pressure causes the plane to lurch and fall, and about air turbulence which causes the wings of a plane to "flap". What seems odd about this case is the total radio blackout.

This was an anomaly that had also struck students of
UFOs or flying saucers, who had been creating extraordinary theories ever since that day in June 1947 when a
pilot named Kenneth Arnold saw nine shining discs moving
against the background of Mount Rainier in Washington
State. The flying-saucer enthusiasts now produced the
interesting notion that the surface of our earth has a
number of strange "vortices", whirlpools where gravity
and terrestrial magnetism are inexplicably weaker than
usual. And if extra-terrestrial intelligences happened to
know about these whirlpools, they might well find them
ideal for collecting human specimens to be studied at leisure
upon their distant planet ...

Ivan Sanderson, a friend of Gaddis's and a student of
earth mysteries, felt that this was going too far. His training
had been scientific, so he began by taking a map of the
world, and marking on it a number of areas where strange
disappearances had occurred. There was, for example,
another "Devil's Triangle" south of the Japanese island of
Honshu where ships and planes had vanished. A corre-
spondent told Sanderson about a strange experience on a
flight to Guam, in the western Pacific, when his ancient
propeller-driven plane covered 340 miles in one hour,
although there was no wind — about 200 miles more than
it should have covered; checks showed that many planes
had vanished in this area.

Marking these areas on the map, Sanderson observed
that they were shaped like lozenges, and that these
lozenges seemed to ring the globe in a neat symmetry,
running in two rings, each between 30°C and 40°C north
and south of the equator. There were ten of these "funny
places", about 72°C apart. An earthquake specialist named
George Rouse had argued that earthquakes originated in a
certain layer below the earth's surface, and had speculated
that there was a kind of trough running round the central
core of the earth, which determined the direction of seismic

activities. Rouse's map of these seismic disturbance areas corresponded closely with Sanderson's "lozenges". So Sanderson was inclined to believe that if "whirlpools" really caused the disappearance of ships and planes, then they were perfectly normal physical whirlpools, caused, so to speak, by the earth's tendency to "burp".

Sanderson's theory appeared in a book entitled *Invisible Residents* in 1970. Three years later a female journalist, Adi-Kent Thomas Jeffrey, tried to put together all the evidence about the Bermuda Triangle in a book of that name, printed by a small publishing company in Pennsylvania. It was undoubtedly her bad luck that her book failed to reach the general public. For one year later in 1974 Charles Berlitz, grandson of the man who founded the famous language schools, once again rehashed all the information about the Bermuda Triangle, persuaded a commercial publisher, Doubleday, to issue it, and promptly rocketed to the top of the American best-seller lists. It had been twenty years since the disappearance of Flight 19, and ten years since Vincent Gaddis invented the phrase "Bermuda Triangle". But Berlitz was the first man to turn the mystery into a worldwide sensation, and to become rich on the proceeds.

Berlitz's *Bermuda Triangle*, while highly readable, is low on scholarly precision - it does not even have an index. One reason for its popularity was that he launched himself intrepidly into bizarre regions of speculation about UFOs, space-time warps, alien intelligences, chariots of the gods (à la von Däniken) and other such matters. And among the weirdest of his speculations were those concerning the pioneer "Ufologist" Morris K. Jessup, who had died in mysterious circumstances after stumbling upon information about a certain mysterious "Philadelphia experiment". This experiment was supposed to have taken place in Philadelphia in 1943, when the Navy was testing some new device whose purpose was to surround a ship with a powerful magnetic field. According to Jessup's

informant, a hazy green light began to surround the
vessel, so that its outlines became blurred; then it vanished
- to reappear in the harbour of Norfolk, Virginia, some three
hundred miles away. Several members of the crew died;
others went insane. According to Jessup, when he began to
investigate this story, the Navy asked him whether he
would be willing to work on a similar secret project; he
declined. In 1959 he was found dead in his car, suffocated
by exhaust gas; Berlitz speculates that he was "silenced"
before he could publicize his discoveries about the experiment.

And what has all this to do with the Bermuda Triangle?
Simply that the Philadelphia experiment was supposed to
be an attempt to create a magnetic vortex, like those
suggested by Sanderson, and that (according to Jessup) it
had the effect of involving the ship in a space-time warp
that transported it hundreds of miles.

Understandably, this kind of thing roused sceptics to a
fury, and there were suddenly a large number of articles,
books and television programmes all devoted to debunking
the Bermuda Triangle. These all adopted the common sense
approach that had characterized the Naval authorities in
1945: that is to say, they assumed that the disappearances
were all due to natural causes, particularly to freak storms.
In many cases it is difficult not to agree that this is indeed
the most plausible explanation. But when we look at the
long list of disappearances in the area, most of them never
even yielding a body or a trace of wreckage, the explanation begins to sound thin.

Is there, then, an alternative which combines common
sense with the boldness necessary to recognize that all the
disappearances cannot be conveniently explained away?
There is, and it rests on the evidence of some of those who
have escaped the Bermuda Triangle. In November 1964, a
charter pilot named Chuck Wakely was returning from
Nassau to Miami, Florida, and had climbed up to 8,000 feet.

Catastrophes

He noticed a faint glow round the wings of his plane, which he put down to some optical illusion caused by cockpit lights. But the glow increased steadily, and all his electronic equipment began to go wrong. He was forced to operate the craft manually. The glow became so blinding that he was dazzled; then slowly it faded, and his instruments began to function normally again.

In 1966, Captain Don Henry was steering his tug from Puerto Rico to Fort Lauderdale on a clear afternoon. He heard shouting, and hurried to the bridge. There he saw that the compass was spinning clockwise. A strange darkness came down, and the horizon disappeared. "The water seemed to be coming from all directions." And although the electric generators were still running, all electric power faded away. An auxiliary generator refused to start. The boat seemed to be surrounded by a kind of fog. Fortunately the engines were still working, and suddenly the boat emerged from the fog. To Henry's amazement, the fog seemed to be concentrated into a single solid bank, and within this area the sea was turbulent; outside it was calm. Henry remarked that the compass behaved as it did on the St Lawrence River at Kingson, where some large deposit of iron - or a meteorite - affects the needle.

Our earth is, of course, a gigantic magnet (no one quite knows why), and the magnetic lines of force run around its surface in strange patterns. Birds and animals use these lines of force for "homing", and water-diviners seem able to respond to them with their "dowsing rods". But there are areas of the earth's surface where birds lose their way because the lines somehow cancel one another out, forming a magnetic anomaly or vortex. The *Marine Observer* for 1930 warns sailors about a magnetic disturbance in the neighbourhood of the Tambora volcano, near Sumbawa, which deflected a ship's compass by six points, leading it off course. In 1932, Captain Scutt of the *Australia* observed a magnetic disturbance near Freemantle that deflected the compass 12°C either side of the ship's course. Dozens of similar anomalies have been collected and documented by an American investigator, William Corliss, in books with titles like *Unknown Earth and Strange Planet*. It was Corliss, who pointed out to me the investigations of Dr John de Laurier of Ottawa, who in 1974 went to camp on the ice-floes of northern Canada in search of an enormous magnetic anomaly forty-three miles long, which he believes to originate about eighteen miles below the surface of the earth. De Laurier's theory is that such anomalies are due to the earth's tectonic plates rubbing together - an occurrence that also causes earthquakes.

The central point to emerge from all this is that our earth is not like an ordinary bar magnet, whose field is symmetrical and precise; it is full of magnetic "pitfalls" and anomalies. Scientists are not sure why the earth has a magnetic field, but one theory suggests that it is due to movements in its molten iron core. Such movements would in fact produce shifting patterns in the earth's field, and bursts of magnetic activity, which might be compared to the bursts of solar energy known as sunspots. If they *are* related to earth-tensions and therefore to earthquakes then we would expect them to occur in certain definite zones, just as earthquakes do. What effects would a sudden "earthquake" of magnetic activity produce? One would be to cause compasses to spin, for it would be rather as if a huge magnetic meteor was roaring up from the centre of the earth. On the sea it would produce an effect of violent turbulence, for it would affect the water in the same way the moon affects the tides, but in an irregular pattern, so that the water would appear to be coming "from all directions". Clouds and mist would be sucked into the vortex, forming a "bank" in its immediate area. And electronic gadgetry would probably be put out of action ...

All this makes us aware why the "simplistic" explanations of the problem - all those books explaining that the

mystery of the Bermuda Triangle is a journalistic invention
– are not only superficial but dangerous. They discourage
the investigation of what could be one of the most
interesting scientific enigmas of our time. With satellites
circling the earth at a height of 150 miles, it should be
possible to observe bursts of magnetic activity with the
same accuracy that earth tremors are recorded on seismo-
graphs. We should be able to observe their frequency and
intensity precisely enough to plot them in advance. The
result could not only be the solution of the mystery, but the
prevention of future tragedies like that of Flight 19.

The Titanic

The Titanic, the "unsinkable" ocean liner that rammed an
iceberg on its first voyage, has become a symbol of human
vanity. In fact, the 46,329-ton monster almost never made it
to sea. On its launch at Southampton in 1912, it narrowly
avoided crashing into another liner, the "New York", when
that ship's mooring ropes inexplicably snapped. Weirdly,
the situation was repeated a few minutes later, when yet
another ship threatened to break its moorings as the
enormous Titanic passed by.

After a brief call at Cherbourg, the Titanic went onto
Ireland, and left Queenstown harbour on the evening of
Thursday, 11 April, steaming out into the Atlantic towards
America, the huge turbine engines driving her on at 22
knots. The captain, Edward Smith was confident; the 2,206
passengers and crew happy and excited by the facilities of
this floating palace and engineering marvel. Most of all,
they felt secure; the ship had fifteen transverse bulkheads
running its whole length to prevent water spreading in the
unlikely event of a leak. The ship even had a double bottom.
So confident were the owners, that the Titanic carried

> The record for the shortest maiden voyage ever
> must be that of 'Daphne', a four hundred and
> sixty-ton steamer, launched on 3 July 1883. She
> rolled down the ramps into the water for the
> first time and promptly rolled over and sank,
> drowning the one hundred and ninety-five
> workmen on board.

insufficient lifeboats for the number of people it was
conveying.

The sea continued to be calm and the skies clear,
though very cold. The temperature dropped during the
early morning of 14 April, and a radio message was
received by the Titanic to watch out for icebergs;
apparently, they were floating much further south than
normal. Just before midnight, with many of the passengers asleep, the look-out suddenly gave the shout that
there was an iceberg directly ahead. In vain they tried to
swing the ship to miss the mountain of ice; it scraped
along the side, and then slipped past them into the night.
Below the water-line, the invisible eight-tenths of the
iceberg's bulk had driven through the double-thickness of
the hull.

The Captain ordered the water-tight doors to be closed,
and the ship was brought to a halt. Water was pouring in.
Few of the passengers thought that anything abnormal had
happened, so gentle had the collision seemed. Whilst the
Captain tried to ascertain the extent of the damage, the
stewards quelled the fears of those passengers who both-
ered to inquire why the ship had stopped. Some passengers
started having a snowball fight with bits of snow the
passing berg had deposited; one man reputedly waved
his whiskey at a passing steward and asked him to go and

see if their was any ice on board. By the time the Captain realized the extent of the damage, and that the unsinkable Titanic was still taking on water in spite of her safety devices, it was thirty-five minutes after the collision. He finally ordered a distress signal to be sent and the lifeboats to be uncovered. The stewards began to wake the sleeping passengers, telling them to put on life-belts and go to the boat-stations. Most did as they were told, but some, thinking it was merely a drill, refused to leave the comfort of their cabins.

The sea was calm as a dark mirror. Most people, standing on the side of the Titanic still experienced no sense of danger; they only saw the gentle waves lapping the sides of the ship fifty foot below. They could not understand why they should have to forsake the security of this castle for the frail lifeboats.

It was women and children first. The boats were loaded, but not lowered. The Captain had heard that the distress message had been picked up by the Carpathia, which was only sixty miles away; it could be there within a matter of hours. The Titanic might be able to stay afloat until it arrived.

Then the bows began gradually to sink into the water, and everyone understood the awfulness of their predicament. The life-boats were finally dropped into the sea; some were only half full. Many women refused to leave their husbands, and decided to stay and die with them. On the deck, people continued to behave in a calm, detached manner. A group of the ship's musicians started playing "Nearer My God to Thee". Some of the men joined in as they stared after their wives and families slowly drawing away from them. Every officer and able-bodied sailor stayed on board.

The three-hundred yard long ship, her lights still blazing, began to dive bow first into the sea, her stern lifting out of the water. Captain Smith finally gave the order to abandon ship. It was two hours after the collision. He himself made no attempt to leave. He stayed at the bridge, and went down with the Titanic. The rest flung themselves overboard into the icy waters as the Titanic became almost vertical. Then her lights went out and she slid down under the surface of the waters, sucking many of the floundering survivors with her; 1,403 passengers and crew, mostly male, died. Among them was the American millionaire, John Jacob Astor. By 4 a.m., the Carpathia had arrived, and managed to rescue those in the lifeboats. With the Carpathia came another ship, the California, which had been less than ten miles away, and had failed to respond to the Titanic's distress rockets. For the rest of his life, the Captain struggled to defend his actions.

The Titanic was eventually found, and attempts were made to raise her. A whole wealth of film and fiction has been built around her fate, and items retrieved from her were recently auctioned. The controversy surrounding the California's Captain continues; his surviving family still maintain his innocence. The Titanic continues to make headlines seventy-five years after the tragedy.

The Herald of Free Enterprise

Ordinary car ferries lack the romance of trans-Atlantic liners, and most people would not seriously consider the thought of anything drastic happening to them as they pop across the Channel or North Sea to the Continent. Yet, in the five years of 1978-1983, there were no less than 1,352 serious accidents in the waters of the North Sea. In spite of this, the operators of the Herald of Free Enterprise continued to cut corners in pursuit of lower costs and tighter schedules, as it ran from Dover to Zeebrugge in Belgium and back.

Catastrophes

It had become something of a habit to set off with the bow doors, through which the cars were loaded, still open. In March 1987, the Herald of Free Enterprise set off from Zeebrugge to Dover, weighed down with more than the requisite number of passengers and a hold full of vehicles. The ferry was known to lean over slightly already. Now it was worse than usual. Just outside the harbour, a wave broke through the partially closed doors and flooded the car decks. This tipped the balance and the ferry rapidly capsized. The awful accident, due almost entirely to negligence, killed one hundred and ninety-three. It was further exacerbated by the disclosure that the ferry was carrying a cargo of illegal toxic waste.

The Best and the Worst

Under the extreme conditions of a disaster, humanity displays the best and worst it is capable of. In the midst of chaos "women and children first" is the traditional imperative. When the Titanic sank, the stories of the courage many showed in the face of inevitable death

---

A two hundred and fifty-foot excursion steamer – the General Slocum – caught fire on a day trip up New York's East River in June 1904. It was a sunny day and the boat was overloaded with mothers and children. It had recently had a new coat of highly inflammable white paint, which enabled the fire to spread rapidly over the wooden body of the boat. When it had finally burned down to the waterline, 1,021 were dead.

The worst ferry accident – and the worst peace-time naval catastrophe – occurred off Manila in the Phillipines at Christmas 1987. A vessel crowded with people collided with an oil tanker and sank in flames, killing at least 2,000 people. As the ship was operating illegally, no-one will know the true number. Only twenty-six survived. Neither the tanker nor the ferry could radio for help as they did not have radio-licenses, and there were no life-jackets or life-boats. In a series of accidents during 1978 and 1979, nearly seven hundred Vietnamese 'boat people' were drowned when their overloaded ships met with disaster.

moved the world. Sixty years beforehand, the passengers of another ship had shown even greater composure and discipline in terrible circumstances.

The ship was the 'Birkenhead', a steam-powered troop-ship transporting British Regiments to South Africa. On 26 February, 1852, the ship hit an uncharted rock whilst rounding the Cape of Good Hope. There were about six hundred and eighty on board, of whom fifty were women and children. The remainder were soldiers and officers of the 74th Highlanders, led by Major Alexander Sexton. In addition, the ship was laden with horses.

The initial collision had already caused dozens of the troops to be drowned as they slept below decks. Major Sexton ordered the survivors on deck, and in one of the more remarkable displays of courage seen, the soldiers stood silently to attention as the women and children were loaded into the life-boats. The ship was sinking rapidly and leaning, but they continued to stand until the

Catastrophes

> The Empress of Ireland, an unglamorous,
> adequately equipped and competently run liner
> mysteriously collided with a Norwegian collier
> in May 1914, off Canada. Within fourteen
> minutes it had sunk, taking with it 1,012
> ordinary people, many of them immigrant
> families. No satisfactory explanation was ever
> found for the collision.

evacuation of the women and children was complete and
the horses were driven overboard to give them a chance.
Only then, at the order from Major Sexton, did they break
ranks and try to save their own lives. But the ship broke up,
and four hundred and eighty-eight of the soldiers died.

In complete opposition to this gallantry, was the occasion when nearly all the fatalities were women and children.
This happened on 1 April, 1873. The White Star Liner
'Atlantic', under the command of the rash and incompetent
Captain Williams, was wrecked on rocks off the coast of
Nova Scotia. Williams, who knew the perils of the area, had
refused to consult charts or maps and had become utterly
lost in the bad weather. In the panic, the male passengers
deserted their families and tried to escape by climbing up
the rigging, taking the boats, or struggling along a line that
had been passed ashore. Their behaviour was shocking.
There were five hundred and sixty deaths. Of the four
hundred survivors, not one was a woman.

Chapter Ten

Sporting Tragedies

S ome of the. catastrophes that reverberate longest in the
memory of the public and leave the deepest scars are those
where days of leisure and celebration go terribly wrong, where
values are completely reversed and grief replaces happiness. What
starts hopefully as a day to remember becomes an occasion which
cannot be forgotten, for all the wrong reasons.

Soccer Madness

L arge crowds in small areas spell danger, whether
caused by fire, disorder or plain bad management. In
the last few years, Britain has seen a number of appalling
tragedies involving its football fans at Bradford, at Heysel
in Belgium and at Hillsborough in Sheffield. The worst
tragedy in a football stadium in Britain prior to this awful
spate was at lbrox Park, the home ground of Glasgow
Rangers on 2 January, 1971. The match between them and
their traditional rivals Celtic was going badly. With only
minutes to play, Celtic still led 1-0. Many of the Rangers
supporters among the 80,000 strong crowd started to leave
the ground early. Pouring down the steps and out of the
tunnels, they heard a vast roar from those still watching, as
Rangers equalized. Immediately, thousands changed their
mind, turned around and rushed back to catch the last few
moments of the action. As they fought to get back in,
others were still streaming out, the force of the crowd
pushing them on. The two forces collided, neither faction

A solitary cross with a poem and roses attached amongst thousands of floral tributes at the "Kop-End" of Liverpool's soccer stadium in memory of those who died at Hillsborough.

retreated, and by that time individuals had no control over their movements. The momentum crushed those in the middle with horrific force. Restraining railings burst, and bodies fell and were trampled on. In the melee, sixty-six people were asphyxiated, while others in the ground were completely ignorant of the massacre going on a few yards away. Cries of panic and pleas for help are drowned under chanting and applause at matches.

1985 was a dreadful year for British sport. The first catastrophe struck on Saturday, 11 May in Bradford. The home club were in with a chance of promotion to the Second Division, and the occasion had a distinct air of anticipated celebration about it.

Bradford's ground was old and wooden, and under the floors of the stands lay the accumulated rubbish of years. When they came to sift through the wreckage, long withdrawn currency was found, which showed that the trash had been gathering for fifteen or twenty years. Shortly before half-time, someone dropped a lighted watch or a cigarette butt which fell through a gap into the midst of this kindling. There, a small fire began to smoulder, which spread under the seating. Suddenly it burst out, and within minutes flames had soared up to the roof. They swooped across it to engulf the whole stand.

Not understanding the potential danger, many spectators just watched, thunderstruck. They were uncertain what to do. For those in the midst of the blaze, a series of errors contributed to the disaster. The fire extinguishers, which in the past had been used by vandals as weapons, had been removed to avoid any repetition. Then, when they tried to escape via the gates at the rear of the stand, they discovered these had been locked to prevent non-ticket holders obtaining entry. The tarpaulin stretched above the stand to give shelter from sun and rain proved to be flammable. It fell and clung to spectators, turning them into human torches. All the while, the TV cameras, which had come to film the football, filmed some of the most shocking scenes ever broadcast on television. Those who survived did so by running onto the pitch.

Fifty-six died, among whom were several fathers and two children. One eleven-year-old died along with both his father and grandfather.

It was a mere fortnight later that the second blow fell. The European Cup Final between Juventus and Liverpool was to be staged on the neutral territory of the Heysel Stadium in Brussels. The already bad reputation that British football fans enjoyed was not enhanced by their behaviour before the match. It was drunken and boorish, and scuffles between groups of fans broke out long before the match started.

Bearing in mind that violent conflict with supporters of the opposite side seemed to have become second nature to British fans, it was sheer foolhardiness to place a block of Juventus supporters at the end of the ground reserved for the Liverpool faction. There was a neutral area between the two groups, but tickets for this had found their way onto the Belgian Black Market, and had been unscrupulously sold onto some of the British. The Liverpool supporters spilled over from their own area into the neutral zone, and picking up speed, charged the adjacent Juventus fans, breaking through barriers and tearing off bits of metal to use as weapons.

The attack forced the Juventus fans down against the concrete terrace walls. One of these was already unsafe, and promptly collapsed; bodies piled up and over it. The police piled in with truncheons drawn, laying about them and generally adding to the panic and horror. Fans escaped by fleeing onto the pitch, where fighting continued, and in the crush of bodies and mangled wreckage on the terraces, thirty-nine people were killed. It was forty-five minutes before medical assistance arrived, a time in which the situation was out of control and beyond salvation. Of those that died, thirty-three were Italian, one of whom was only ten years old. The only Briton to die was a casual visitor, attending his first game. Twenty-two Liverpool supporters subsequently faced criminal charges in Belgium, and English clubs were banned from European competitions.

The most recent chapter in British soccer catastrophes opened on 15 April, 1989. It was a warm and sunny Spring day. Liverpool were due to meet Nottingham Forest in the semi-final of the FA Cup. They were to play on neutral ground, at the Hillsborough Stadium in Sheffield, the home of Sheffield Wednesday Football Club. The two teams had played here before under the same circumstances. The match was a sell-out, with 54,000 fans expected. It was going to be a good match, and an excellent day's entertainment. The Police presence was heavy, and every effort was made to ensure fans arrived in town and travelled to the ground with the minimum of fuss. As with security surrounding all matches, it was coordinated like a military operation. What the Police didn't want to see were clashes between rival fans outside the stadium, and the purchase of tickets from touts which might result in the two groups mixing inside.

Kick-off was scheduled for 3 p.m. It was Police practice to avoid delaying the kick-off unless under exceptional circumstances - if for example, bad weather meant that large groups of fans might be delayed and would arrive late. Otherwise, delay only meant that the schedule for moving supporters in and out of town would be upset, disrupting the lives of the local inhabitants.

There was a certain amount of drinking after local pubs opened in the morning, but the greatest problem the Police had was caused by fans committing "trespass to urinate" in gardens. Although the turnstiles opened early, it was noticeable that few of the Liverpool fans were entering the ground in good time. At the Leppings Lane Entrance,

Catastrophes

behind the West stand where the Liverpool fans had been
segregated, a heavy Police presence was under no pressure
to hurry as they searched supporters for drink and weapons.
The terrace areas were divided up into pens, separated by
high wire mesh across steel frames. These pens theoretically
allowed Police and stewards to divide and control the
distribution and flow of the crowd, to segregate trouble
makers and to prevent mass movement which could lead to
stampedes. At midday it was decided by the Police that all
the pens on the West Stand would be available to fans from
the beginning; they would not herd them into any particular one, but leave it to the fans' sense and choice.

By 2 p.m., with kick-off an hour away, the Nottingham
Forest sections of the ground were filling up rapidly, whilst
the West Stand remained half empty; some pens had almost
no spectators in them, though those with the best view,
pens three and four which were directly behind the goal,
were proving much more popular than others. From turnstile figures the Police worked out that only 12,000 ticket-
holders had passed through. Going on previous experience,
it should have been 20,000 by this time. Somewhere out
there were a lot of Liverpool fans, and time was running out
for them to get in before kick-off.

Suddenly, the crowd outside began to build up dramatically. The area between the turnstiles and the perimeter
gates became congested. The Police on foot and on
horseback had trouble manoeuvring. The Police still believed that it would be possible to get them all in by 3 p.m.,
and Superintendent Duckenfield, who was in overall command decided that the kick-off would not be delayed.

Whilst the crowd continued to swell outside the turnstiles, those fans who had got in continued to press forward
into pens three and four. More people were arriving than
were being let through, as the task was beyond the capacity
of the turnstiles. The Police on foot become too squashed to
exert control, and were worried by the fact that the crowd

100

The worst crowd disturbances ever seen at a football match turned into a full scale riot with casualties on a battle-field scale. In 1966, Argentina and Peru were playing a 'friendly' fixture in Lima, the capital of Peru. The 45,000 crowd were largely Peruvian supporters and as their team was trailing 1–0 towards the end of the match, they were none too happy when the referee disallowed a goal that would have equalized the score. Fans invaded the pitch intent on beating up the referee, but were beaten back by police. More invasions followed, and the referee suspended the game. This precipitated a charge by the angry mob, and the players and referee fled to the dressing rooms whilst the police foolishly tried to tackle the crowd with the use of guns and tear-gas. Panicked, afraid and still angry, 45,000 people rushed for the exits, trampling and crushing hundreds. Outside the stadium, those who had escaped went on the rampage, looting, smashing and burning. By the time it was all over, three hundred were dead and five hundred injured.

was now tailing back through the perimeter gates and onto a road. As kick-off drew closer, supporters, some of whom had been drinking, lost their good humour and became angry and frustrated. Packs of young men who arrived were determined not to miss the kick-off and began to push their way forwards. A gradual forward momentum started, like water at a dam. Some women and children began to faint. Pleas to the crowd to stop pushing were in vain. The Police could not restrain them; use of force would have caused a massacre in such a confined space. The Police could not even check for drink and weapons, they were soon desperately trying to move people through into the ground. By 2.45 there were 5,000 people in a vast crush around the turnstile. And once inside, they continued to aim directly ahead, for pens three and four. As these were by now excessively full, a tail back began to form to the entrance to these, preventing people from proceeding to other pens. This is the point at which the situation teetered on the verge of becoming a dreadful tragedy. If only the kick-off could have been delayed until control had been restored. But the clock kept ticking, and those arriving at the back selfishly charged -in, having no conception of the effect their actions were having.

So bad was the crush, that the Police officer in charge considered the situation unmanageable, and requested of Superintendent Duckenfield that the exit gate adjacent to the turnstiles should be opened to allow the crowds in. Otherwise he feared that someone was going to die. Duckenfield did not respond immediately, and procrastinated whilst matters deteriorated. When he finally agreed, and the gate was opened at 2.52 p.m. 2,000 fans rushed through the open gate in five minutes. Some probably did not have tickets. Some went left or right to the side pens, but the majority went straight ahead. and tried to pile into pens three and four, which were now potential death-traps. Down at the front, against the wire, people were already choking.

When the teams came onto the pitch, there. was a huge forward rush from the crowd, which increased the murderous pressure at the front of the overflowing pens. Many were now crying out for the gates at the front to be opened to let them escape. But their cries were lost in the cheering, and the Police could not distinguish waving from drowning. The Police were trained and drilled to deal with

A couple sit and grieve among the rows of empty seats at Liverpool's Anfield stadium, following the Hillsborough disaster.

Catastrophes

June, 1955. The Le Mans Grand Prix, the classic race; twenty-four hours of gruelling driving at phenomenal speeds. A glamorous, grimly competitive and dangerous occasion, particularly in the days before crowd safety was a major consideration. This particular race is about to change all that. British driver Mike Hawthorn laps another Briton, Lance Macklin, and then pulls back in front of him as he prepares to slow down for a pit-stop. Behind Macklin comes the French driver, Pierre Levegh, who is about to be lapped by the World Champion, Juan Fangio. Macklin finds he is too close behind Hawthorn; he can't slow down in time. He pulls over to the left, and Levegh smashes into his rear. As Fangio squeezes past to safety, Levegh's car leaves the track. It doesn't skid; it flies, fifteen foot in the air, lands like a projectile in a crowd of spectators and explodes. The rear axle is fired off and decapitates those standing nearby, while blazing oil and petrol and a shrapnel of white-hot engine components are shot all over the place. The result is horrendous. Eighty-two people are dead, plus Levegh. Motor racing stops altogether for months, and, too late for the victims, the safety of spectators becomes an issue.

disturbances. When the front gate to pen three was forced open, they closed it, and surmising that it was a potential pitch invasion pushed back those who were trying to get out. Some lucky ones did escape, and were redirected into

A young boy on crutches stands before the "Kop-End" goal mouth at Anfield stadium following the Hillsborough disaster.

the side pens. Others started to try and climb the wire onto the pitch but were driven back by the Police. Most of those in the crush were unaware of the game. Their arms were pinned to their sides, they were jammed against fences, gates and crush barriers or each other and some were slipping down onto the ground. Those at the rear continued to drive forward in their urge to see.

At 3.04 p.m. a shot from Beardsley playing for Liverpool struck the Nottingham crossbar at the other end of the ground. In expectation and excitement, the crowd at the West end surged forwards like a tide, and a crush barrier, which had been breaking some of the lethal momentum in pen three, collapsed. Many went over with it and never got up. In pen four things were almost as bad. The pressure of the surge did not ease off. Those crushed at the front and underfoot were already dying. Within four minutes they would suffer brain damage from lack of oxygen, and beyond that, death. The Police, who had up to this point still thought that they had a potential pitch invasion brewing, realized the truth. The officer on the scene sent word to Duckenfield that the game would have to be stopped, and then, without waiting for an answer, he ran out onto the pitch and collared the referee himself, who stopped it immediately. It was 3.05 p.m., and on the terraces, ninety-five people had died.

They opened the gates at the front of the pens. There was a ridge of bodies along the front of pens three and four. The gateways were so congested with the dead, dying and injured that each body had to be disentangled by the police, who were dreadfully confused and shocked, not knowing what they were supposed to be doing. Those called to assist came prepared for crowd violence, and were turned into stone by what they saw; the victims were blue with asphyxiation, their mouths open and eyes staring, incontinent, vomiting. The crowd poured through the gates, some stopping to help and adding to the confusion, others falling and adding to the carnage. Some turned on the Police, kicking, spitting and abusing those who they blamed for the catastrophe. Everywhere the press photographers, in pursuit of pictures of the dead and injured snapped their faces at point blank range, interfering with the rescue work, showing no compassion and no remorse.

Only three of the victims were over fifty; the majority were aged between twenty and twenty-nine. Among them were seven women. All had died of asphyxiation, and in addition four hundred were seriously injured. It was a tragedy brought about by a series of errors, and although the Police took a string of short-sighted decisions, the irresponsible and wickedly selfish behaviour of sections of the crowd was also to blame. It was not a new scenario. In 1946, thirty-three people were crushed to death at Bolton in Lancashire under similar circumstances, when the crowd

In March 1976, a cable car carrying forty-three
skiers crashed two hundred feet into a dry river
bed near Cavalese in northern Italy, when its
cable snapped; the only survivor was a fourteen-
year-old girl.

outside at the start of a game forced its way into the
ground, destroying a wall, knocking down barriers, and
ploughing into the trapped stationary spectators inside.
Then, also, an irresistible force met an immovable object
with fatal results.

The Fastnet Yacht Race

The Fastnet Yacht Race began in 1925, and quickly became
one of the major events in world sport. It has a five hundred
and seventy-three mile course, which takes yachts from
Cowes on the Isle of Wight, over to the south of Ireland
and the Fastnet Rock and then back to the English coast at
Plymouth in Devon.

In 1979, the twenty-eighth competition, there were three
hundred and three vessels of widely differing size compet-
ing, coming from twenty-one nations with a total number
of crew in the region of 2,500. They set off for Ireland on 11
August, and sailed straight into some of the worst weather
ever seen off the British coast. It was worse, some survivors
claimed, than the many hurricanes they had experienced in
far more exotic places. A force-ten wind and waves running
as high as fifty foot from crest to trough tore into the fleet.
Some of the big boats, although crippled, were able to turn
back. Not the smaller ones, who were tossed like match-

Catastrophes

wood, turned upside down and frequently sank. The crews, taking to the life-rafts, faced hypothermia and discovered they would have stood more chance sticking to the wreckage of their boats than entrusting themselves to the unstable inflatables. The rescue services distinguished themselves with repeated acts of heroism, as did the competitors themselves. As a consequence of this only fifteen were drowned, but of the three hundred and three hopeful boats that set off, only eighty-four finished.

Chapter Eleven

Under the Volcano

A volcano is a hole or opening in the Earth's crust through which a mixture of super-heated molten rock and gases are forced to the surface, and in the process they tear the Earth's surface into the familiar cone-shape. There are distinctive areas of volcanic activity in the world, and most of the violent business takes place along the edges of tectonic plates, where immense portions of the Earth's crust meet. The plates knit and shift ceaselessly, and forty miles under the Earth's surface, the mantle of soft rock melts and rises under the impetus of barely imaginable frictional forces. This is how new lands are created. In 1963, Surtsey, an island off the coast of Iceland was born in this way. After several days of eruptions beneath the Atlantic, a ridge of land had formed, which rose out of the water on 15 November. For months eruptions continued, and by the end, there was a new island, only a mile square, topped with a huge volcano.

It's hard to be rational when faced with an angry volcano, and they were frequently worshipped as Gods. If it was an active volcano, it was a violent God, and if the volcano was quiet, it was evidence that he or she might be appeased and would continue to let people live and work on the slopes, so long as the mountain's almighty force was revered. Recently, when Mount Etna erupted again in Sicily, not only was prayer tried to avert the flow, but many locals who were forced to flee their houses left offerings of food to the volcano in the hope of satisfying its obvious hunger.

Perhaps the most violent eruption of all, and one that profoundly changed the face of civilization, took place over 3,000 years ago on the Greek Island of Thera, north of Crete.

Catastrophes

Only a sliver of what was once Thera remains above water; where its crescent shape encloses a vast bay there once stood a volcano 5,000feet high. When this erupted it completely disappeared in the violence of its own explosion. It left a crater, 1,300 feet deep. It was this eruption that archaeologists were later to connect with the destruction of the ancient, highly cultured and sophisticated civilization of the Minoans. Located on the north coast of Crete, this people would have been removed from the face of the earth within minutes of the eruption, as a wall of water two hundred feet high rushed down on their towns. What remained of the Minoans was scattered far and wide. It has also been speculated that the clouds of volcanic ash may have spread to Egypt, in time to pick up a starring role as the thick darkness among the plagues that Moses brought on the Pharaoh. The explosion has also been connected to the Atlantis myth, the story of a lost island, the centre of a vanished civilization.

Mount Vesuvius

The people of the sprawling city of Naples on the west coast of southern Italy have had a long and turbulent relationship with their local volcano, which remains the most famous in the world. It continues to be active nearly 2,000 years after its most famous performance when it burned and buried the towns of Pompeii and Herculaneum. All around the region are scattered lesser smoke-holes and safety valves for the big mountain. One of these, Solfatara, a low crater, is accessible by the public who can have the rare experience of skirting their way around a lake of bubbling sulphurous mud. Not far away is the small and dormant Monte Nuovo, which when it sprang into life a couple of hundred years ago, vapourized an entire village which had optimistically been built on its summit. The area reeks of sulphur.

Under the Volcano

Vesuvius has been active for 10,000 years or more, but in Roman times it had been dormant for centuries and was not thought to be a threat. Towns sprang up around it and on its slopes, and the Bay of Naples was a popular holiday resort. Then, in AD 79, it blew its top.

Pompeii had become the commercial and agricultural centre of the region and had a population of around 20,000. It was buried beneath pumice stone, the form that cooled lava takes. On the other side of the mountain, mud covered Herculaneum, and the towns and their buried inhabitants were forgotten for 1,500 years. Then, treasure hunters stumbled onto the remains of Herculaneum in 1738. Pompeii surfaced ten years later. The discoveries electrified the cultural world with its renewed interest in classical civilization and architecture. The sites became a sensation. Extensive excavation revealed that much of the towns had been almost perfectly preserved, right down to the meals that people were about to eat when the lava, mud and ash poured on them. Over 2,000 skeletons were discovered at Pompeii, and it proved possible to take plaster casts of the holes in the rock where bodies had once been. These extraordinary models re-create a world on the point of death. Men, women, children and animals cower and huddle with hands and cloths over their mouths to try and keep out the poisonous gases streaming off the pumice from pene-trating their lungs.

The most famous account of a volcanic explosion was made at this time. It is the record that the Roman writer Pliny the Younger made of his father's death. His father was a keen naturalist, and was always too interested in phenom-ena to be frightened. Holidaying at Misenum on the Bay of Naples, his interest was attracted by a vast cloud rising over the mountain, and shortly afterwards, hearing from a friend that she was in danger of being engulfed in her house, he took a ship and set out across the Bay to Stabiae, intent on a rescue mission. He never returned, and perished, along with thousands of others in a maelstrom of ash, pumice, fire and mud. The following day, his son and family left Misenum, which was being shaken and rocked like paper. They were followed by a vast crowd of terrified locals:

> ". . . night came upon us, not such as we have when the sky is cloudy, or when there is no moon, but that of an enclosed room without lights. You might hear the shrieks of women, the screams of children and the shouts of men, some calling for their children, others for their parents, others for their husbands, and seeking to recognize each other by the voices that replied; one lamenting his own fate, another that of his family; some wishing to die from the very fear of dying; some lifting their hands to the gods: but the greater part convinced that there were now no gods at all, and that the final endless night of which we have heard had come upon the world ... a heavy shower of ashes rained upon us, which we were obliged every now and then to stand up and shake off, otherwise we should have been crushed and buried in the heap ..."

Vesuvius has regularly been erupting and taking lives since 1631. It's due for another explosion shortly.

Krakatoa

The eruption of the Pacific island of Krakatoa in 1883, one of the best documented of natural catastrophes, is one of the most devastating displays of force ever witnessed. That 36,000 died may seem an horrendous statistic; but the violence was so great that the figure looks comparatively modest. The final explosions were

November 1985. The prosperous, sleepy town of
Almero, Columbia, died at the hands of a
volcano called the Nevado del Ruiz. The
eruption of this three-cratered, 5400-metre high
monster was only small but it melted eight per
cent of the vast ice cap, sparking off a towering
river of mud that engulfed the houses of
Almero. Among the 25,000 dead were 8,000
children, and among these was a girl of twelve,
Amraya Sanches, whose desperate struggle to
stay alive became the centre of world attention.
Perched on the dead body of her aunt, she
endured for three days stuck up to her neck in
mud, whilst continuous attempts were made to
free her. She finally slipped into a coma and
died, saying "God is calling me now."

mistaken for loud gunfire 3,000 miles away, and shook
remote parts of Australia 2,000 miles away. Thirteen
cubic miles of material were ejected into the heavens, of
which four cubic miles rose into the atmosphere in the
form of fine dust and produced spectacular red and green
sunsets throughout Europe and North America for
months afterwards. Krakatoa was actually a group of
small islands in the Sunda Strait between Java and
Sumatra. The largest was five miles long and had three
volcanic cones, Rakata, Danan and Perboewatan. North
of this larger island were three smaller ones. All four
islands were uninhabited. The volcanoes had long been
considered extinct, having last erupted two centuries
beforehand. In May of 1883 it, or they, belched into
life, sending a cloud of smoke and flame seventeen miles
into the air, and raining pumice down on the surrounding

ocean. At first, the continuous eruption was spectacular but mild, and various scientists hurried to study it and were impressed with its awesome beauty:

> "From the middle of this dark and desolate landscape, the epitome of total destruction, a powerful column of smoke of indescribable beauty drifted over the sea, several tens of metres in width at its base. The column was hurled into the sky with the crash of thunder to a height of 3000 feet ..."

The eruption continued at this level for some weeks, by which time most of Perboewatan had disintegrated. As there seemed to be no real threat to life in the immediate area, and no escalation on the part of Krakatoa, interest waned. Then, in late August, the explosions grew more threatening, building up to a remarkable climax on 26 and 27 August. There were no witnesses as to what actually happened to the islands on those days, because at 1 p.m. on 26 Sunday, a cataclysmic series of blasts put out the lights over the Sunda Strait for the next three days. Ships passing in the distance saw the gloom and flashes of fire ahead. The remains of Perboewatan were sent flying from the main island. A ship's captain, who found himself a mere ten miles away when all hell broke loose, recorded in his log:

> ". . . the blinding fall of sand and stones, the intense blackness above and around us, broken only by the incessant glare of various kinds of lightning and the continued explosive roars of Krakatoa, made our situation a truly awful one ... chains of fire appeared to ascend and descend between the sky and Krakatoa, while on the southwest side there seemed to be a continued roll of balls of white fire; the wind ... was hot and choking, sulphurous ..."

8.32 a.m., Washington USA, 18 May, 1980.
America's pet volcano, Mount St Helens erupted
with a rumble that measured 4.1 on the Richter
Scale. It shot a cubic mile of earth and ash into
the sky, and caused widespread destruction,
flattening hundreds of miles of forest and
clogging lakes with debris.

Krakatoa went into its death throes around midnight on
the 26th. It had sprayed out all the melted rock in its
subterranean reservoir, but was still rocked by ejaculatory
explosions. A void began to form, and Krakatoa started to
collapse in on itself, accompanied by an unholy series of
pyrotechnics which landed three foot of ash on that ship ten
miles away and heated the copper fittings until they were
untouchable. The crew were all struck by electrical dis-
charges. The noise echoed across the world; the shock
waves sped around it seven times, and in an apocalyptic
explosion at 10 a.m. on the 27th, three-quarters of Krakatoa
vanished beneath the sea.

As it disappeared, it created a huge whirlpool, and
generated tsunami, "tidal waves", over one hundred feet
high, which raced off towards the coasts of Java and
Sumatra. At Merak, inhabitants climbed to the top of a
one hundred and thirty-foot hill to escape the waters, which
still managed to reach them. Towns, fields, hills and forests
became open sea, and very few from the surrounding
communities survived. All that remained of the main island
of Krakatoa was half the cone of Rakata. Two of the smaller
islands had grown, and one had vanished altogether.

In 1927, rumbling under the water indicated the arrival of
the offspring of the volcano, and the following year, the
"Child of Krakatoa", a one hundred-foot volcano, rose up

out of the water. It is as yet, only a baby, with a whole, happy life ahead of it.

Mount Pelee and Soufriere

The eruption of Mount Pelee was a showcase for a new weapon in Nature's arsenal, the dreadful "nuee ardente" the burning cloud. This occurs when magma, boiling rock, super-charged with steam and emerging under tremendous pressure hits a weak point in the chimney of the volcano. The wall of the cone cannot withstand this force and bursts. A super-heated jet of magma, dust and steam mixed with poisonous gases squirts out and burns everything in its path. It doesn't have to start a fire to kill; the heat can literally cook people.

In 1902, St Pierre was the largest town and principal port on the Caribbean Island of Martinique. It was a peaceful little community with narrow, winding streets and quaint old houses. Five miles to the north was Mount Pelee, which means the 'Bald Mountains' which had long been dormant. Inside its crater, at a height of 4,500 feet was a lake. The area was very picturesque and was a favourite picnicking spot.

Early in April 1902, smoke and rumbling started in a ravine on the side of the mountain, but no-one took much notice. There were a few minor earth tremors, and a couple of days later there was a minor explosion which showered the town with ash. Another crater, on the side of Mount Pelee, grew a new cone, and a lake of sulphurous water formed. The disturbances grew worse, and as disquiet and anxiety spread among the local populace, many closed shop and fled. Making a classic mistake, the authorities sought to prevent panic and assured them there was no real danger. They continued to insist there was no cause for alarm even when the new lake boiled over and sparked a mud flow which reached the sea, burying a sugar factory and causing waves in the bay that were big enough to flood some parts of the town. The indigestive rumbles grew louder, and by 7 May were echoing around the Caribbean. On the neighbouring island of St Vincent, the dormant volcano La Soufriere heard the noise of its brother and also woke up. A column of steam, 30,000 feet high came shooting out of its crater, and a day later came its eruption culminated in an awesome "nuee ardente" which frazzled everything in its path and killed 1,500.

This neighbouring eruption had a curiously calming effect on the inhabitants of St Pierre, who illogically thought that the catastrophe they had been awaiting had happened, but to others. Many returned to their houses. Shortly before 8 a.m. on 8 May, Mount Pelee reached a critical state, and its top blew to pieces. The "nuee ardente" emerged, travelling at over 100mph, at a temperature of 2,200 degrees, and annihilated St Pierre and its inhabitants in two minutes flat. Of the 30,000 present, two people survived. Every house in the vicinity was razed to the ground; even stone walls crumbled. For hours afterwards the heat coming from the pile of ashes was too great for ships to approach the harbour. An officer aboard a ship offshore from the island, the *Roraima*, recalled the event:

"... The side of the volcano was ripped out, and there hurled straight towards us a solid wall of flame. It sounded like a thousand cannons. The wave of flame was on us and over us like a lightning flash. It was like a hurricane of fire, which rolled in a mass straight down on St Pierre ... wherever the mass of fire struck the sea, the water boiled and sent up clouds of steam. I saved myself by running to my state-room and burying myself under the bedclothes ..."

Catastrophes

The memoirs of the two known survivors in the town
sound like recollections of Hiroshima. In the afternoon,
when the volcano was spent, a French priest came into the
harbour on a boat and saw what was left of St Pierre:

> " ... Its ruins stretch before us, wrapped in their
> shroud of smoke and ashes, gloomy and silent, a city
> of the dead. Our eyes seek out the inhabitants fleeing
> distracted or returning to look for the dead. Nothing
> to be seen. No living soul appears in this desert of
> desolation, encompassed by appalling silence ..."

Chapter Twelve

The Nuclear Scenario

T he prospect of nuclear catastrophe has haunted the world for the last fifty years. Robert Oppenheimer, the leader of the Manhattan Project, who created the Atomic bomb, was not joking when he surveyed the scene of the first detonation, and quoting Hindu scripture, said:

"Now am I become Death, the destroyer of Worlds ..."

The Use of Nuclear Power

T hroughout the years of the Cold War, the Earth came close to a holocaust on more occasions than were publicly admitted. In 1956, the American Secretary of State, John Foster Dulles disclosed that America had been on the verge of nuclear war on three occasions over the previous three years. The threat continued in the 1960s and 1970s; political crisis and plain error nearly precipitated the unthinkable. On 6 June 1980, a computer malfunctioned at the centre of the American nuclear web, the North American Defence Command headquarters in the Cheyenne Mountains, Colorado. It wrongly informed the Americans that a Soviet missile strike was on its way. The B52s, laden with nuclear weapons, were sitting on the tarmac with their engines running for twenty minutes, although the mistake was discovered after only three. It was the second such alarm in three days. Thankfully, for the moment, the men thousands of feet under the Cheyenne Mountains are currently spending more time tracking drug smugglers than planning for nuclear war.

The very tangible danger has come from the "peaceful" use of nuclear power; nuclear generating plants are potential bombs; radioactive leaks have long-term effects that are still only partially understood.

The first indication of what the future held happened at the old Windscale plant in Cumbria on the English coast in 1957, when a delicate control process being conducted by scientists went wrong and a cloud of radioactive dust was released from the plant. The staff were evacuated, and attempts made to cool the over-heated uranium rods in the reactor. Civil defence teams were called in to seal the area, and although a fortuitous off-shore wind blew the majority of the dust out to sea, some workers in the plant were contaminated as were nearby cows, whose radioactive milk was then tipped into the sea, passing the contamination onto marine life and thereby back into the human food chain. Over the years, local people began to show higher incidents of cancer and evidence of radioactivity in their thyroid glands.

Twenty-two years and many "minor" leaks and hushed up incidents later, the Three Mile Island nuclear power plant in Harrisburg, Pennsylvania USA caused what was, until Chernobyl, the worst known peacetime nuclear accident. On 29 March, 1979, a combination of human error and stuck valves allowed the fissioning core of the reactor, normally submerged safely beneath the water, to become exposed to air. The highly radioactive rods that constituted the core of the reactor, went into "meltdown", and large quantities of radioactive gas were released. For three days there was a distinct danger that the swelling bubble of radioactive hydrogen, twenty-eight cubic metres in size would explode, or that total "meltdown" would result. Either way, although officials tried to play down the public's alarm, a nuclear catastrophe threatened to wipe the population of Washington off the globe. All residents within a five mile radius were evacuated, and others were advised to stay inside their homes. Technicians managed to reduce the size of the gas bubble to 1.3 cubic metres by the end of the third day, but it was weeks before they could claim the situation was no longer dangerous.

On 5 April, 1986, a group of Russian nuclear engineers began a programme of tests on the RBMK boiling-water reactor at Chernobyl in the Soviet Union, about eighty miles north of Kiev in the Ukraine. Having been shut down for tests, the power level in the reactor was allowed to fall beneath its stable safety point, of twenty per cent, and this instability led to a power surge which disintegrated the nuclear fuel rods into fragments of superheated ceramic. This evaporated the water into steam, which in turn caused a violent explosion, and cracked the reactor. Thirty fires erupted. The fifteen metre flames created an inferno, which not even the courage of the fire-fighters could quell, many of whom effectively gave their lives, dying of radiation-poisoning later. The cracked and blazing reactor reached a temperature of 2,000 degrees fahrenheit at its core, spewed one hundred million curies of radiation into the atmosphere, and narrowly avoided going into total meltdown. Helicopters eventually were used to smother it with 5,000 tonnes of sand, clay and chemicals. In the aftermath, 617,750 acres of topsoil were removed and buried, but although the radiation had spread across Europe, the Soviet authorities at first refused to admit that the accident had happened. The area itself had not been evacuated for thirty-six hours after the catastrophe. The inhabitants of Chernobyl itself, all 40,000 of them, remained in their homes being poisoned for six days. Every single European government underestimated the extent of contamination; in Britain it was only two years after Chernobyl that it was discovered, or admitted, that hill farms in the north were positively glowing with radiation, and that for years, the public had been consuming products which were highly contaminated.

Official Soviet estimates for the effects were ludicrously low; thirty-one dead, one thousand injured, perhaps another 6,000 dying from cancer in the next seventy years. Western estimates put the potential fatalities nearer 250,000, besides the untold damage done to agriculture and the environment. Recently, ex-President Gorbachev has confessed that the figures the Russians gave for the estimated damage caused by Chernobyl were only a fraction of what they truly anticipated.

Chapter Thirteen

Paths of Destruction

Tropical storms are cyclones, or rotating wind systems, which are called hurricanes or typhoons if their wind velocity exceeds 75mph. Storms in the Atlantic tend to be called hurricanes, whilst those in the Pacific are known as typhoons. The origins of these storms is not precisely known, but they emerge from a combination of the eastern trade winds and the hot surface of the oceans. Most tropical storms originate in the area called the "Doldrums", which moves season to season but which basically straddles the Equator. The ascent of warm, moist air from the ocean is followed by the formation of rain clouds and a subsequent drop in the atmospheric pressure. It is around this core of low pressure that the wind begins to rotate, forming a vortex of cloud and water that can rise up to 40,000 feet and have a diameter of two hundred miles. The storms move at about 15mph, and in the northern hemisphere they drift inexorably northwest, and in the southern hemisphere, southwest, bringing devastating winds, and torrential rains in addition to the vast storm waves they can generate. The wicked little cousins of these masters of destruction are tornadoes, often called "twisters", which are also funnels of spiralling air. They originate over land rather than sea, and are much smaller in diameter. The most violent tornadoes occur, as everybody who has seen "The Wizard of Oz" will know, on the Great Plains of the USA, as well as in Russia and Australia. They are one of the wonders of nature. Rarely more than four hundred metres in average width, but sometimes a mile high at the top and tiny at the bottom, they are pillars of wind, given shape by the debris they suck up into their vast funnels that connect the earth to the heavens. They writhe and rise and dip like snakes. Inside the funnel, the wind spins at

500mph, and when the bottom of the pillar touches any structure, it rips it to pieces. The damage they create can be amazingly local. Objects and people only yards away from the path of a twister can survive untouched. They are accompanied by awesome electrical storms, with lightning striking twenty times per second. A small twister can have more electricity whirling round inside it than all that produced by the entire generating capacity of the USA. Their power to whisk away houses is no exaggeration; one carried off a church steeple and deposited it fifteen miles away. Wooden houses, as favoured by prairie inhabitants, have been moved two miles.

Hurricanes, Cyclones, Tornadoes and Typhoons

Hurricanes and typhoons come in seasons, hurricanes occurring between June and October. One of the worst hurricane seasons in history occurred in the Caribbean in 1780. Eight hurricanes of terrible intensity struck the islands, and three of them within the first three weeks of October. The first of these hit the port of Savanna-la-Mar in Jamaica on the 3rd, sending waves of awesome size rushing in to inundate the town. On the 10th, the "Great Hurricane" arrived in the Caribbean, hitting Barbados with winds of 150mph. Barely ten houses were left standing on the island. From there it scythed its way across half-a-dozen of the other islands, leaving twenty thousand dead in its wake. The third hurricane came shortly afterwards, and was most notable for destroying the Spanish fleet of Admiral Solano, which was on its way to attack the British at Pensacola. He had been planning the assault for a long time, but the only joy he had was to have the hurricane named after him.

The typhoons of the Pacific and Asia are much more widespread and frequent. In the Bay of Bengal, where they experience the most violent tropical storms in the world, typhoons are, confusingly, known simply as cyclones. It is these that have so plagued Bangladesh, which lies at the head of the bay and is most exposed. It was a cyclone that, in 1970 actually helped to give birth to the country, which at that time was a part of Pakistan. On the night of 12 November, a massive wave swept across the low-lying islands off the coast, drowning upwards of 200,000 people, and destroying livestock and buildings. It then sucked back out to sea taking its prey with it. In the aftermath, the inhabitants of Bangladesh faced disease and starvation. The cyclone occurred on the eve of an election, and the indifference of the Pakistan government to the tragedy and their inefficient distribution of the international aid supplies were seen as indicating how little they thought of the poor of the Bay of Bengal. This resulted in the election of a radical party, The Awami League, which in turn finally led to independence.

Chapter Fourteen

Flood and Fire

F ire in confined spaces is one of man's greatest enemies, let
alone fire on a grand scale, moving in a wall across the
landscape or devouring a city. But fire can often be controlled, or
will burn itself out. Nothing can extinguish the power of
hundreds of billions of tons of water on the rampage; it can
take years for floods to subside. There are two types of floods;
those which are accidental, that result from the failure of a dam
for example, and those which are tidal or seasonal, which happen
when rivers become too full and burst their banks as a
consequence of rain or high tides.

The Johnstown Deluge

O n 31 May 1889, Johnstown, Pennsylvania USA
entered American mythology as the town that
was wiped off the map by a flood. About twelve miles
upstream, and several hundred feet above the town was the
South Fork Reservoir and Dam. Once part of the Pennsylvania canal system, the reservoir had become a private
hunting and fishing club. It was about three miles long, and
was thought to be the largest reservoir in the country. The
old dirt dam was not well constructed, and had leaked and
spilled before. It had been rebuilt, but its central section still
contained no masonry, and it had no discharge pipes. In an
alarming development, its spillways which would allow
excess water to escape, had been plugged to prevent the
loss of fish. The residents of Johnstown, who had endured

> The Indus and Ganges rivers in Asia run through
> very mountainous regions and are liable to
> become blocked by natural dams of rock and
> other debris. During the winter of 1840-41, a
> landslide from the Nangu Parbat Mountain fell
> into a stretch of the Upper Indus, which had
> become blocked by natural rubbish, and formed
> a lake three hundred yards deep and forty miles
> long. The landslip raised the level of the water
> above the blockage, and 2.5 billion yards of
> water formed twenty-seven foot high waves and
> engulfed an army battalion encamped down the
> base of the mountain.

modest flooding before, were fairly blasé about the potential danger.

During May, heavy rains fell, and after two days of particularly heavy downpours, the dam began to come under acute pressure. There was already some flooding in other parts of the county, and the managers of the dam began to feel anxious. They dug emergency slipways in the hope of relieving the build-up, and telegraphed a warning to the inhabitants of Johnstown. The residents weren't unduly alarmed, and went about their business. In the middle of the afternoon on the 31st, the dam finally gave way; a small breach rapidly widened and the flood began its journey, down the Conemaugh Valley to Johnstown. On the way, it engulfed several villages with a wall of water one hundred and twenty-five feet high, travelling at 50mph. As it rolled down the valley, with a noise like incessant thunder, it picked up and bore along houses, factories, entire families and whole forests. It took only forty minutes to drain the entire reservoir. This is how one man, standing above its passage saw it:

"I was horrified at the sight that met my gaze up the valley. It seemed as if a forest was coming down upon us. There was a great wall of water roaring and grinding swiftly along, so thickly studded with trees from along the mountain sides that it looked like a gigantic avalanche of trees ... the scene was beyond the powers of language to describe ... it was ruin no human agency could avert, the flood rolled over houses and people, burying them out of sight entirely."

Johnstown was the largest settlement by far in the valley. It was swamped. Many of the buildings in the town were stone, which did not save them from being entirely destroyed when the huge wave, armed with debris, tore into the town. The people were caught by surprise, and within seconds 2,200 of them disappeared forever beneath the waters. So violent was the flood that the water carried debris down the valley as far as Pittsburgh, seventy-five miles away. Of, Johnstown, only two roofs could still be seen breaking the surface of the lake that had closed over it.

The Chinese Floods

When it comes to "natural" flooding, there are no greater destroyers than the rivers which flow across the great plains of China. Principal among these are the awesome Huang Ho

---

In 1963, an avalanche poured into the lake above the Vaimont Dam in Italy, creating vast waves which crested the dam and poured down on people living below, 2,600 of whom drowned.

---

and Yangtze Rivers. The Huang Ho, the "Yellow River" is known as "The Ungovernable", and "China's Sorrow". It takes its name from the yellow earth, a mixture of sand and clay that it picks up and then deposits as it journeys from the Tibetan Highlands across the North China Plains to the Yellow Sea. The River slows down as it crosses the plains, and it is here that the dirt is deposited. It fills the river-bed, and causes it to overflow its banks. This flooding is vastly magnified when heavy rains fall.

In 1889, heavy downpours in the Honan Province caused the Huang Ho to burst through dykes at the city of Cheng-Chou, which it drowned in minutes. The mighty flood poured eastwards towards K'ai Feng, destroying six hundred villages. In the plain below K'ai Feng, it covered another 1,500 settlements, and then spread into the neighbouring province of Anhwei, from which it took two years for the standing floods to recede. The damage was staggering, and was followed by a famine; as these low-lying provinces are the rice-producing areas of China, hunger reached beyond the immediate area affected. In the flooding alone, somewhere between two and seven million died.

This catastrophe was repeated in 1931, where the Huang Ho once again overflowed its banks, and killed approximately four million. Only a few years later, the mighty river again went on the rampage, breaking its banks a little further down its 2,900 mile course, and leaving at least ten million homeless. Nothing can resist the Yellow River, which frequently changes its course with impunity. In the middle of the last century, it moved its mouth north by two hundred and fifty miles.

As if this were not enough, the Yangtze has also cruelly deluged the interior of China. The Yangtze is China's longest river. Connecting the heartland of China with the Pacific Ocean, it flows for 3,400 miles, large sections of which are dyked, as it flows above the level of the plains of

Catastrophes

Towering infernos do happen. On February, 1974, the Joelma Building in Sao Paulo, Brazil, an office skyscraper constructed out of a choice selection of inflammable materials caught fire. The flames erupted on the eleventh floor, and within seconds had cut off six hundred and fifty people. As the fire spread upwards, those escaping it fled ahead of it, until they were so high that there was no means of rescuing them, as the fire service ladders could not reach that far. The only alternative to being burned to death was to commit suicide by jumping. After four hours the flames were brought under control, by which time two hundred and twenty people had died.

the "rice-bowl" provinces. There are 7,000 square miles of lakes connected to it, which hopefully provide reservoir space in the event of flooding. But this system cannot cope with the effects of torrential rain across all of it.

In September, 1911, the Yangtze flooded and completely swamped the provinces of Hunan, Hupeh and Anhwei along with the city of Shanghai. Nearly 100,000 drowned, and another 10,000 died of hunger. In 1954, the heaviest rainfall for a century swelled the river until, where it flooded, it drowned an area twice the size of Texas with a wall of water nearly one hundred feet high; across twenty-seven million acres, 40,000 people were drowned.

The Great Fire of London

The fire that destroyed the old centre of the City of London in 1666 remains one of the most famous of catastrophes. In spite of the small death toll, the fire has continued to grasp the imagination of successive generations. It followed in the wake of the Plague, consuming a city that was putrid with the dead and dying, cleansing as well as destroying; in its wake a new London emerged.

On 1 September, a fire started at the King's bakery in Pudding Lane near London Bridge. There had been no rain for weeks and the wooden houses were tinder dry. Fanned by a strong easterly wind, the flames spread rapidly through the warren of streets and the narrow winding lanes lined by houses which leaned outwards, their upper stories almost touching across the filthy, crowded passages between them. Efforts to bring the fire under control by using the "bucket brigades" quickly failed. By the morning of the 2nd, three hundred houses had collapsed into burned out shells. Panic began to spread among the population, who tried to leave the city and clogged up all the available routes, making it even harder to gauge the extent of the growing conflagration let alone do anything about it. Bells rang, carts crashed, people poured down to the Thames in an attempt to escape by boat, and those who had not buried their possessions threw them into the river in the hope of retrieving them later. The chaos was exacerbated by the arrival of thousands of tourists from the villages outside London, who had come to have a look at the disaster.

The most famous account of the fire was given by the diarist Samuel Pepys, who was Secretary to the Navy Board. He went down to the Tower of London in order to get a good view of proceedings, and from which point he observed that the whole area north of London Bridge was now in flames; it looked as if the Bridge, which was lined with houses, was soon to be burned. He hurried off to tell

Catastrophes

the King, Charles II, the "Merry Monarch", who ordered that all houses in the path of the fire should be pulled down to try and create a fire-break, beyond which it would not cross. They started doing this with hooked poles, tearing at the ridge beams, and then using teams of horses, but the fire outstripped them. By 4 September, half of London was in ruins. Even the King was reputedly spotted passing buckets of water in an attempt to extinguish the flames. Houses were blown up with gunpowder to try and isolate the fire. The sound of explosions started rumours of a French invasion and fuelled the panic. In the city, as refugees poured out, country folk poured in, doing a roaring trade in wagons and carts, which they hired or sold for half the value of the goods being transported. Old St Pauls, the vast gothic cathedral, that was the teeming and latterly seedy heart of the city, was finally caught in the fire. Charles II had recently ordered that it be renovated, and the immense and sprawling building was covered in scaffolding which collapsed as the flames took and ate their way into the wooden beams. The acres of lead on the roofs melted and boiled, gushing down through the gargoyles like water, and the great cathedral caved in.

St Pauls was the fire's last major victim; it threatened but did not reach the Tower, and was finally brought under control, by which time only a fifth of London was left. Virtually all civic buildings had been destroyed, along with 13,000 private dwellings. Amazingly, only six people were known to have died as a direct result of the fire, but hundreds of thousands were homeless.

In the wake, a demented French watch-maker called Hubert confessed to having started the fire deliberately, and was rapidly hanged, before it was realized that he could not have done it, as he was not even in England when it occurred. The idea that it was a deliberate act of terrorism persisted, however. A number of scapegoats were blamed; the Dutch, because England was having one of her interminable wars with Holland, the French, whom they have never trusted because, in spite of their proximity to England they persist in speaking a foreign language, and the Roman Catholics who were a reliable scapegoat for most blows of fate. A monument was erected on the spot the fire broke out, in 1677. A two hundred-foot column, it originally bore an inscription, which was later deleted, blaming the Fire of London on a Catholic Conspiracy. By 1671, much of Christopher Wren's principal rebuilding of London had been completed.

The Great Chicago Fire

In 1871, Chicago, although less than forty years old, had in this short period become one of the liveliest cities in the world, a thriving centre for the cattle and grain trade centred on the plains. Six miles long by three miles wide, and bounded on the East by Lake Michigan, Chicago had the distinction of being a city made largely of wood; even the sidewalks were planked.

Fire was a considerable hazard, and a common occurrence. The city boasted that it possessed the finest Fire Department in the country, which was not saying a great deal. This was a city of 300,000, and in spite of its seventeen horse-drawn fire engines and twenty-three hose carts, the department was not sufficient to cope with a serious conflagration. There were a few telegraph alarm boxes posted around the city, but the Fire Department's most reliable method of locating fire was the look-out, stationed on top of the courthouse who had a decent view of the city.

The Summer and early Autumn of 1871 were very dry, and there was a spate of fires in the weeks leading up to 8 October. On 7 October, the Fire Department had fought a blaze for hours, winning an heroic victory and were entitled to feel exhausted at the end of the day, as well as

Catastrophes

Fire turns theatres into death-traps. These days strict regulations require every inch of fabric in a theatre to be chemically fireproofed; several dreadful incidents have shown what can happen in the absence of decently enforced regulations. In 1903, the elegant, newly constructed Iroquois Theatre in Chicago caught fire during a matinee performance of a musical comedy. The majority of the large audience were women and children, of whom six hundred and two died. The fire broke out when sparks fell from an improperly enclosed arc lamp. These ignited the inflammable cloth border of the scenery. The cast fled out of an exit backstage, and the oxygen coming in through the open door created a lethal draught which forced a huge tongue of flame under the inflammable safety curtain and into the packed auditorium. Every fitting and fixture inside the theatre was inflammable; heavy, plush seats, drapes, wall-hangings and wood everywhere. There were thirty-five exits from the auditorium, of which thirty-two were blocked, and all exits were hidden behind heavy curtains. The sprinkler and ventilation systems did not work and none of the staff had been given any training in the fire-drill. To add to the ingredients for catastrophe, the 1,602 licensed capacity of the theatre had been vastly exceeded by the greedy management; there were 1,830 people packed in. Most could not get out of the auditorium, and hundreds of bodies piled up in front of the locked exit doors.

> This was not the worst theatre fire. Seventy
> years beforehand, to the day, a fire at a theatre in
> St Petersburg killed seven hundred; a few years
> later 1,670 died in a theatre fire in Canton, China.
> On 8 December, 1881, the world premier of
> Offenbach's 'Tales Of Hoffman' at the Ring
> Theatre in Vienna was interrupted by a fire that
> began on stage and ended by killing at least eight
> hundred and fifty members of fashionable
> Viennese society.

considering they had good reason to celebrate. Either way, the dashing men of the Fire Department were a bit slow in responding to the events of the following day.

This was the moment at which Mrs O'Leary's cow entered American history. Mrs O'Leary lived in De Koven street on the west side of the city, an area settled in by Irish and German immigrants. It was in her barn, at about 9 p.m., that her cow was popularly believed to have kicked over an oil lamp.

The fire spread quickly from the barn, fed by favourable winds, and soon had several houses blazing. Someone did try to use the alarm signal box nearby, but it failed to work. The look-out spotted the smoke and flames rising, but not until the fire had been going for half an hour or so. He called the Fire Department, and reported it, but quickly realized that he had given them the wrong location. Unfortunately, when he tried to change his instructions, the telegraph operator on the exchange would not pass on the message, insisting that it would only confuse the firemen.

When the fire-engines located the blaze, it was already serious, but was at least restricted to a single block. The wind carried it, however, and by midnight, and with all the Fire Department's resources employed, there were twenty city blocks burning. It was a dark, windy night, the only light coming from the ever-spreading flames. Panic spread,

Catastrophes

Disco and club fires, breaking out in crowded, badly lit, badly ventilated and frequently unlicensed premises have proved lethal in recent years. Many deaths are due to the inhalation of toxic fumes from modern furniture containing synthetics. The tragedy is often heightened by the young age of the victims. The Cinq-Sept Club in the small town of St Laurent du Pont, near Grenoble in France was merely a barn. It had no license, no water, no telephone and no windows. The only exit was the turnstile the customers came in by. When a match fell on a cushion one night in 1970, it was fortunate that the time was late and the club only half full. But of the one hundred and fifty teenagers who were still dancing, one hundred and forty-four were killed, principally overcome by poisonous fumes. There was a similar tragedy at the Stardust Ballroom in Dublin on Friday 13th, 1981. The dancing was due to go through into Valentine's Day. At 1.30 a.m., someone slashed a seat and set fire to it. The hall became an inferno and forty-eight of the young revellers died.

and order collapsed. In the early hours of the morning, the flames jumped the Chicago River into the slum and red-light areas of Franklin, Jackson and Conley's Patch, where the inhabitants, many the worse for drink became crazed with fear and obstructed the fire-fighters' progress. The fire moved northward into the main business district; it burned down the new marble courthouse, which had been claimed to be fireproof. By dawn it had reached the Lake where it was busy burning ships. The speed of the spread shocked everybody. It was hoped that it would spare the houses of the prosperous, protected by the River on the north side of the city. But, early on the 9th, a burning plank flew across the water and landed on the roof of the waterworks, which promptly burned down, thus cutting off supplies to the fire-fighters. There were no resources left to send to the area, and people just had to stand and watch it burn furiously, the temperature rising to 3,000 degrees at the centre of the conflagration.

The fire burned on into the night, when rain began to fall. By the following day, people could emerge and look at what was left of Chicago. The heart of it, an area four miles long and a mile in width had been razed. The death toll was low, with only two hundred and fifty to three hundred perishing. Still alive were the O'Leary family, whose house was untouched. They had to hide in their attic for days, besieged by an angry mob demanding they be lynched. Patrick O'Leary, the husband of the cow's owner became the particular target of their hatred, and was eventually forced to leave town in disguise. It is unclear whether the cow survived or not.

Chapter Fifteen

Off-Shore Drama

*H*appening neither on land nor sea, not on a boat nor an aeroplane, but on man-made, mini-worlds in some of the harshest conditions on earth, oil-rig disasters have a particular resonance, as the victims are so isolated, and often so helpless.

Oil Rig Tragedies

The first of two recent tragedies happened in 1980, when the four-year-old "Alexander Kielland", a drilling rig which had been converted into an accommodation platform for workers on the adjoining "Edda" rig, turned over in dreadful weather, one hundred and sixty-four miles off Stavanger in Norway, far into the North Sea.

It was in March, with winds driving at 130mph into the rig's structure and whipping up enormous waves. On board the rig were two hundred and thirteen men, most of whom were bedding down for the night. The rig, unlike many drilling platforms which can hoist anchor and drift with the swell in monstrous seas, was attached permanently to the neighbouring "Edda", and was beginning to take the buffeting badly. Moreover, it still had a two hundred-tonne derrick on its deck, which made it top heavy and liable to tip over. Which, in the middle of the night, is what happened. Without prior warning, it suddenly gave in to the sea and tilted over at forty-five degrees. It later transpired that the fifth supporting leg of the rig had snapped ten metres under the waterline. The whole design had never been properly

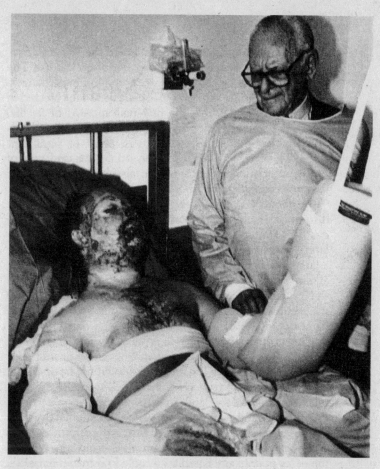

A survivor of the Piper Alpha oil rig disaster being visited by Dr Armand Hammer, head of the rig's owners Occidental Oil.

tested for potential metal fatigue. Within fifteen minutes, the vast, 10,105 tonne structure was hanging upside down, and the men sleeping on-board had been flung into the freezing sea, and one hundred and twenty-three of them were lost. After the disaster, it was discovered that another five rigs were suffering from many of the same flaws.

Catastrophes

The most recent catastrophe, on board the "Piper Alpha" rig in the North Sea, was caused by explosion and fire. The Piper Alpha was thought by some to be the most dangerous platform in the North Sea. It had stood unprotected in the corrosive waters for the first nine months of its life, before the anti-corrosion system was commissioned. Underwater inspections revealed a vast array of significant faults. There was an explosion on it in 1984, and several deaths in accidents. Sabotage had also been attempted. It was not considered to be a lucky rig.

At about 9.45 p.m on 6 July 1986, there was a major disruption to the gas processing system. A safety-release gas flare started to burn furiously, but its flame was much larger than usual. Despite efforts to control the flow of gas, a huge leak built up, and at 9.58 p.m, with most of the crew aboard watching the film "Carrie", a high-pitched scream of ripping metal was followed by an almighty explosion in the mechanic's workshop. Diesel leaked out and fuelled the flames. A series of explosions followed, which destroyed both the rig's communications systems and its control system; there was no way of issuing either instructions or warnings, and even the fire pumps could not be operated. As the fires began to spread unchecked over the rig, men followed the safety drill in the absence of any other instructions, and assembled at various points, unaware of the seriousness of the situation. Inside the rig, those who were trapped tried to keep themselves from inhaling the fumes, or poured any liquid they could find over themselves in the hope of saving themselves from burning. Some found a crate of tomatoes and sat there squashing them over their faces in a effort to keep cool. Some were already dead from fumes. At 10.20 p.m., a major gas-riser jet running through the centre of the rig blew, and began to release hydrocarbon gas at the rate of 1,800 pounds per square inch. The effect was devastating. A fireball enveloped the rig and flames rose seven hundred feet into the sky. The only option the crew had was to jump into the water. Some rescue ships had arrived, but they could only watch the inferno. At 10.52, the remaining gas pipelines connected to Piper Alpha erupted in an even greater fireball, which burned millions of cubic feet of gas; so powerful was the fire, that some ships left the area for fear of being burned. The flames continued to blaze for the next four days. There were two hundred and thirty men aboard, and one hundred and sixty-seven of them died.

Chapter Sixteen

Financial Catastrophes

D id their greediness or egomania get the better of them? There is one fundamental objective for a swindler and that is to make as much money as possible without worrying how, and who, they go about getting it from. They are very confident people, who do not tolerate being told what, and what not, to do or care who suffers along the way – and that is usually their downfall.

John De Lorean

J ohn De Lorean started his career with seemingly everything going for him. He was General Motors's "Golden Haired Boy" who could do no wrong, and swiftly moved up the corporate ladder into the GM executive suite. He later became famous for his "winged" De Lorean sports car and for his involvement with a string of beautiful women. Little did anyone know that he was set on a course for disaster.

Born in Detroit, "the Motor City", in 1925, the son of a Ford employee, he had cars in his blood. His family was poor – De Lorean once told how he wore the same suit from the time he was twelve until he left college. After graduating from university he decided to try his hand at selling advertising space for the Yellow Pages. The only problem was that the Michigan Bell telephone company published the other Yellow Pages (the original version) and attempted to have De Lorean tried for fraud. He managed to extract himself from his predicament by paying back all of the businesses he had taken money from.

After this experience, De Lorean decided to switch tack and enroled at the Chrysler Institute as an engineering trainee. He did a stint working for the Packard Company for a few years and changed over to GM when they folded. He soon became the youngest general manager of the Pontiac Division, and was later tipped to take charge of the fast-growing Chevrolet Division. Under his management, Pontiac's image was changed from that of a maker of an old lady's car into a racy powerhouse bestseller. He introduced important engineering innovations, such as the overhead cam engine, the concealed windshield wiper, and the radio antenna embedded in the windshield. While De Lorean was head of Chevrolet, nearly 3.5 million cars were made a year - more than any other car company before them. The company went from a twenty-year downward trend to its most profitable years and De Lorean seemed to have the GM presidency in his hand.

By this time De Lorean, who was tall, elegant and handsome, had become obsessed with his appearance and had undergone plastic surgery to make his chin square and rugged looking, as well as a nose job. He also changed other aspects of his life, including divorcing his wife of fifteen years. He started dating beautiful women such as Ursula Andress, Candice Bergen, and Nancy Sinatra, then married Kelly Harmon, the nineteen-year-old daughter of an American football hero. De Lorean later divorced her to marry well-known fashion model Cristina Ferrare, then twenty-three and known as the Max Factor girl.

He radiated immense power and energy to everyone he met and was admired within the automobile industry for his credibility. *Auto News* wrote when he left GM: "Now, more than ever before the industry needs the colour and style of a De Lorean." Others, however, said De Lorean had been in mental and moral decline since he took over

Catastrophes

Chevrolet and had been involved in some shady deals. At this time he also began investing heavily in things such as real estate, oil fields, and football teams. Before taking over Chevrolet, De Lorean was described as portly. But once the phone calls from Hollywood started coming in to this newly powerful man, he became a health freak and lost about 40lbs.

In 1973, De Lorean left General Motors. Rumours abounded that he was asked to leave for taking kickbacks from Chevrolet dealers. GM top management had also reportedly become concerned about both damaging leaks concerning information about new product designs, problems with dealers, and production schedules, and De Lorean's increasingly erratic behaviour. After hiring a private detective to track down the leaks, it was found that they were coming from De Lorean himself. When confronted with this information, the former Golden Boy threatened to go public with other embarrassing documents about the company and they finally settled on an agreement: De Lorean would leave GM with a settlement of a $1 million Cadillac dealership in Florida.

De Lorean then tried to make it in various businesses and failed - with many ending in litigation and questions about his business ethics. The first of these was a business De Lorean started with two of his brothers called Grand Prix Ltd, which franchised race tracks around the US with tiny racing cars. The venture ended with the company filing for bankruptcy in November 1975, and one of his brothers suing him. They were also charged with fraud by a man who was tricked into buying $100,000 of Grand Prix stock.

Next, De Lorean came up with the idea of manufacturing two-seat sportscars with the distinguishing feature of having doors that opened up instead of out, like wings. The car would have a slew of safety features. The idea was not an original one, however. The year before, a man from Philadelphia named Malcolm Bricklin had attempted to design, manufacture and sell a similar car, but failed when it was found that the cars were riddled with problems.

In 1975 the De Lorean Sports Car Partnership was created, with a projection of selling thirty-five cars at $100,000 each. After having difficulties in finding a location to set up his plant, the British government of James Callaghan stepped in and offered the use of Belfast as a site in return for various subsidies. They never investigated his background nor questioned his reasons for leaving his job with GM that had paid him $700,000 a year. The deal was expected to bring sorely needed business to the struggling Irish city, which was one of the poorest areas in Europe. De Lorean cut a deal with the British which gave him $97 million, one-third of which was a grant, with a promise of $20 million more if employment goals were reached. The British government was never to see that money again. In 1980 De Lorean employed 1,000 people and the company was rapidly growing. But soon debts began to pile up and cars were slow to come off the assembly line. The company was in trouble. De Lorean began looking for more investors and new bank loans. Some company funds were allegedly used to finance a personal land deal in California that he was negotiating, and $8.9 million was used to refinance his purchase of a ski-slope snow grooming equipment business in Logan, Utah. He then turned to the British government again, asking for more funds, but was turned down and an audit of the company's books was ordered. De Lorean scrambled to find the money to cover his debts and avoid bankruptcy, and was nearly successful. But he was duped, because the drug deal which was going to save De Lorean's company was a set-up by the US Federal Bureau of Investigation. They convinced him that if he helped them with the deal to import drugs into America, he would receive $10 million working capital instantly and another $50 million on the way. James Hoffman, an old friend of De Lorean's who had turned informer for the DEA set up the deal, which the automobile manufacturer saw as his only hope of rescuing the "dream car". Meanwhile, the FBI agent who posed as the "Mr Big" who would finance the deal for half of the De Lorean motor company, and the banker who would launder the money, were recording every incriminating word spoken by De Lorean - fifty-eight telephone conversations in all were taped. On 19 October 1982, FBI and Drug Enforcement Agency agents arrested him for allegedly selling $16 million worth of cocaine. And they had it on videotape.

De Lorean's defence lawyer, Howard Weitzman, had successfully defended other seemingly hopeless cases: alleged Mafia capos and brutal killers and even got a member of the Manson family off a murder charge - the only one out of the group to go free. The attorney managed to delay the case for seventeen months, then exploited his client's glamour to build public sympathy for him. He eventually convinced the jury that he had been entrapped: the law enforcers had gone beyond permissible measures to seize a suspect and had set up the conspiracy which snared De Lorean. Weitzman also used De Lorean's high-profile wife, Cristina Ferrare, by advising her how to dress and act in the courtroom and sending her to appear on television talk shows and defend her husband. During the trial, Ferrare, who was a born-again Christian, convinced De Lorean to convert to Christianity. Just when the jury seemed ready to give a verdict, he was baptised in his ornamental swimming pool of his 400-acre estate in Bedminster, New Jersey, with Cristina at his side wearing a long white gown. He wore a drip-dry leisure suit.

De Lorean managed to evade jail on a technicality and walked away a free, though considerably poorer, man. He left behind him a pile of debts amounting to more than $250 million, as well as $17.5 million that was never accounted for. The British government was out £84 million, 2,600 De Lorean factory workers were out of a job, and the Northern

Ireland economy - already in a slump - was dealt another blow. In addition to the failure of his empire, his third wife left him.

Horatio Bottomley

Horatio Bottornley was born with the gift of gab, and could charm almost anyone into giving him their money. He rose to become a well-known politician and an expert conman. Born in the East End of London in 1860, he knew early on that he wanted fame, women and a brilliant political career. But making money, and lots of it, was his dream. Bottomley helped start the *Financial Times* and the patriotic magazine *John Bull*, and was later elected to represent Hackney South – a London constituency - as a Member of Parliament. He lived the life of a local squire with his wife in Upper Dicker near Sussex, and kept a series of mistresses all over England.

Bottomley began working as a clerk for a solicitor, then went to work as a shorthand writer at the Law Courts in London. Next, he started a publishing company along with some friends; bought some properties and a printing works in Devon for £200,000 from a friend. He then sold them to the publishing company for £325,000. Bottomley's colleagues charged him with fraud when they found out that most of the properties weren't worth anything - something he already knew. The conman decided to defend himself during his trial, and won, impressing the judge so much by his technique that he was told to think about becoming a lawyer. From one swindle to another: Bottomley's next target was the Australian gold boom. He eventually made a small bundle of money by promoting the gold mines, though his firms habitually failed and he was regularly served with bankruptcy writs. Yet, he never had any trouble finding people to invest in his ventures.

Catastrophes

Bottomley's scheme was to start a company and announce high dividends, then he and his co-horts would sell the shares once their price increased. When the business started to fail, he would create another one and use the new shareholders' money to buy up the old company. In 1912, the conman was forced to resign from Parliament when a bankruptcy case he was involved in was made public. During the war he used his magazine to support Britain's efforts and recruit soldiers. His patience paid off and he was re-elected as an MP for his constituency in 1918. Bottomley operated his last swindle the next year, when he began selling government-issued Victory Bonds through a club to working-class people who couldn't afford the full price of £5. Investors could spend whatever they wanted, with the club picking up the rest of the tab for them. Bottomley, however, was skimming money off the top, and by the time he was discovered he had taken £150,000 of the investors' cash. Within the six months the scheme ran, he had spent most of the money already on paying off debts, horse-racing, and buying and exhibiting a German submarine. He was prosecuted in 1922 for fraudulent conversion of funds and sentenced to seven years in prison. The former millionaire died penniless in 1933.

Robert Maxwell

"Captain" Bob Maxwell lived much as he died - mysteriously and surrounded by publicity. The billionaire press lord's naked body was found floating in the ocean off the Canary Islands, six hours after the crew of his yacht, the Lady Ghislaine, had reported him missing. Circumstances surrounding his death, or the cause of it, are still unknown and may never be discovered, but one thing is known: Maxwell, sixty-eight, was deeply in debt when he died.

Although he was thought to have a fortune of £1.2 billion, making him Britain's eighth richest man when he died, Maxwell in fact left behind a legacy of unpaid bills and crumbling businesses. It was later revealed that the publisher had been making inter-company loans; using the money from his companies' pension funds to cover losses in other companies. The collapse of his empire has left many employees without jobs and hundreds without pensions. Many shareholders have been left with worthless investments. A week after Maxwell's death it emerged that his companies owed banks £758 million, and the value of shares in the businesses had collapsed. Investigators discovered that a total of £297 million was missing, owed to Maxwell Communications and Mirror Group Newspapers, and finally realized the extent to which Maxwell had plundered his companies. After a full investigation it was revealed that total liabilities for the company had risen to £1.8 billion (assets were worth about £800 million), and that Maxwell had taken £245 million from MCC, and £97 million from MGN. Total losses in pensions were £429 million, with bank debts at about £1 billion. Months after his death, investigators were still examining the Maxwell papers to figure out just how much the former press baron had lost.

Maxwell's rags-to-riches story began in Solotvino, Czechoslovakia, where he was born Ludvik Hoch in 1923 to a Hasidic Jewish family of impoverished labourers. As a child Maxwell often went hungry, and only had three years of formal education. He apparently joined the Czech resistance movement against the Nazis when he was fifteen, and later took to selling trinkets to earn a living. He lost most of his family in the Holocaust. As a youth he fled to France where he fought in the French resistance movement and met his French wife Elisabeth Meynard, before he escaped to England.

In England he joined the British Army, became a captain and was later awarded the Military Cross for heroism for fighting in Normandy. A few years later, in 1949, he borrowed money from his in-laws and founded Pergamon Press - a company that imported and distributed German scientific journals in Britain. The business made him a millionaire. In later years he boasted that he launched Pergamon with £13,000 and sold it for £446 million. He later became a world leader in the field of scientific journals and set himself the goal of becoming the world's largest printer.

During this time he and his wife had nine children, among them Kevin and Ian who were just three years apart in age and later came to help their father run his empire. The success of Pergamon enabled Maxwell to win a seat in the House of Commons as a Labour MP in 1964. Four years later he left office after failing to become a cabinet minister due to financial finagling, but was a committed life-long Labour party member. He had been courted by the Conservatives — including ex-Prime Minister Margaret Thatcher — to join their party, but had turned them down. During the 1987 election campaign, he refused to publish a three-page advertisement for the then desperate Tories, making a slew of enemies within the Conservative party.

In 1980, Maxwell once again proved his worth as a businessman, buying the heavily indebted British Printing Corporation and turning it into a successful operation. Maxwell, who was quickly bored, then decided to move into newspapers and book publishing. It took him a while to acquire the newspapers he wanted to buy, but in 1984 he purchased the racy London tabloid, the *Daily Mirror*, and entered into a media war with Australian media baron Rupert Murdoch who owned *The Sun* tabloid. Under Maxwell's leadership, the circulation of the *Daily Mirror* increased from 200,000 to 3.6 million. He also bought a stake in MTV Europe. The *Daily Mirror's* success, however, didn't extend to all his other holdings. The *London Daily*

News, launched in 1987, lasted only five months. In May 1990 Maxwell launched The *European*, a daily European newspaper, after failed attempts to buy the *National Enquirer*, America's biggest selling tabloid, as well as three other American tabloids.

Maxwell loved America and was anxious to move into the US market. He ended up paying huge sums for media properties there in the late 1980s – he paid $2.6 billion for Macmillan Inc. publishers in 1988 – and his expansion into the United States left him heavily leveraged. In February 1991, however, Maxwell indulged himself once more and began making tenuous inquiries into the purchase of the strike-ridden New York *Daily News*. In the years before, Maxwell had regularly phoned the *News's* publisher to ask if the paper was for sale. Until then he hadn't had a chance. When the deal finally went through, with the unions making important concessions, the *Daily News's* headline read "Cap'n Bob bites the Big Apple". Many considered Maxwell a hero at the time – he had saved the *Daily News* from the grave.

Maxwell was legendary for being incredibly hard working – he normally worked 14-16 hour days – and for being incredibly difficult to work for. He liked to rule his employees by fear and demanded that they work as hard as he did. The media magnate would often fire employees at will. He once even fired his son, Ian Maxwell, for failing to meet his plane at Orly airport in Paris. When his helicopter landed at the Daily Mirror building in central London, staff would run through the building sounding the warning, saying: "The Ego Has Landed."

When Russian troops invaded Lithuania in 1990, Maxwell's newly appointed *Daily Mirror* editor Roy Greenslade (a former senior editor at the *Sunday Times*) had his newspaper cover the event. Maxwell rang Greenslade to tell him to cease reporting negatively about the actions taken by Gorbachev, whom he considered a good friend.

Catastrophes

Greenslade understandably objected to Maxwell's interference, pointing out that "news is news". Maxwell responded by saying that Gorbachev would not do anything without consulting him first. Soon after Greenslade was sacked.

Maxwell considered himself a media magnate and enjoyed being compared to publishing giant William Randolph Hearst. He liked to have his ego stroked and would often take would-be calls from the White House while visitors to his office (especially bankers) waited to speak to him. Cap'n Bob liked to believe that he was a powerful and influential world figure and international statesman, and enjoyed the welcomes he received at foreign airports, and the waiving of passport formalities.

He did, however, hold strong ties to the communist leaders, including East Germany's Erick Honecker. He met with him shortly before the Berlin Wall came down, and was later criticized for being a fair-weather friend to the leader. Before Honecker was removed from office, Maxwell described him as having been a reformer all his life.

"I have played a major part in the changes that have taken place in many of these countries, as is best evidenced by the fact that I'm playing a leading part with the new people. Why? Because I have always been a professed, strong anti-Communist," said Maxwell in an interview. He did admit, however, that he had made mistakes in his associations with East European leaders, (in the past he lauded leaders such as Romanian despot Nikolae Ceausescu) but that his mistakes were not in befriending them but in not saying publicly how critical he was of them.

Maxwell also expanded his business interests into Eastern Europe and invested heavily in newspapers there. He travelled extensively and spent at least nine days a month in New York. A committed Zionist, he oversaw an airlift of ailing Soviet Jewish children from the Chernobyl area to Israel in 1990 and later visited them there by helicopter.

All the flying and overwork, along with his being about 90lbs overweight, led to health problems. Although Maxwell suffered from chronic colds, made worse by the partial removal of a lung thirty years ago, he never slowed his pace. Even with all the pressures he was feeling from his business problems, Captain Bob would never have let it show. His strategy was to never panic.

We will never know, however, if that is what Maxwell did on the night of 5 November 1991, when his body was found floating in the Atlantic Ocean. Did the mountain of debt he had built up finally cause him to panic? Or was it an accident? Or perhaps murder ...

According to investigators, Maxwell's behaviour shortly before his demise that night was out of character and strangely indecisive. He unexpectedly decided to take a trip on his yacht to help get over a cold, and did not bring any staff or guests aboard which was unusual for him.

The Lady Ghislaine was a colossal yacht Maxwell owned and operated and often used to entertain and impress his visitors. It had a main stateroom and four decks, and the crew consisted of thirteen and two chefs. The boat could be chartered for about £100,000 per week. Before boarding, guests were asked to take their shoes off.

He boarded the yacht in Gibraltar and planned to take a cruise over the next week to help recover from a cold. He was seen by a crew member on deck at about 4:25 a.m. - about half an hour before the time of death. Maxwell complained that he was warm and the air conditioning fans were switched on. About twenty minutes later he called the bridge and asked that the fans be turned off. He was never heard from again. The next morning, after a phone call from New York for him, Maxwell was found to be missing. That afternoon, after the alarm was sounded and rescue crews were notified, Maxwell's naked body was spotted floating in waters off the Canary Islands.

Catastrophes

Maxwell's widow and eldest son, Philip, arrived to identify the remains, which were then flown to Jerusalem on a chartered jet for burial. The oversized casket containing Maxwell's 286lb body, however, did not fit onto Maxwell's private jet and a larger plane had to be ordered.

Insurance investigators who hold the £20 million life policy on the publisher are still trying to determine exactly how Maxwell died. But an official report issued in February 1992 indicates that they consider suicide the most credible answer. They have ruled out a heart attack, though not completely, because they say if this had occurred he would have been more likely to have fallen down on deck, and are quite certain he could not have rolled from the deck into the sea. Loss adjustors have also excluded the possibility of murder, because, they say, there is simply no evidence to suggest it. One of the reasons they say suicide was the cause of his death is that he was unusually "complimentary and almost amicable towards the crew". The report suggests that it was conceivable that he had reached the conclusion that the collapse of the empire was inevitable. "We wonder whether Robert Maxwell's decision to spend those last days on the Lady Ghislaine, his request that his jet rendezvous with the yacht at sea and his unusually pleasant manner the majority of the time, were brought about by Robert Maxwell's realization that the end of his business career and his flamboyant lifestyle was rapidly drawing to a close," the report says.

Dr Iain West, a noted British pathologist who conducted a second postmortem examination on the body of Robert Maxwell before it was interred in Israel, says his findings suggest that the cause of death was probably drowning.

In the year before he died, Maxwell began selling off his assets in an effort to shrink his debt. When he died his companies were about $4 billion in the red. A few days after he died the sale of Berlitz International, a language training organization, was finalized. The Japanese publishers Fukutake purchased the company for $265 million. Still, this was not enough to save Maxwell Communications Corporation and his other companies from an uncertain future. After Maxwell's death, MCC, which included Macmillan Publishing, Collier's Encyclopedia and Official Airline Guides, was in debt for $2.5 billion. In the 1991 financial year its revenues had been $2 billion. Mirror Group Newspapers, including the *Daily Mirror* and four other British newspapers, was in hock for $583 million with yearly revenues of $792 million. And Robert Maxwell Group Ltd, which comprised the New York *Daily News*, *The European* and the Oxford United Football Club was $1.3 billion in debt with revenues unknown. With all of his holdings, Maxwell was not producing enough money to pay off his loans; he was paying $290 million in interest on the $2.6 billion he had borrowed.

Maxwell liked to describe himself as being not just a hero, but a cult figure. His main strength was his extraordinary courage but his major fault was his intimidation of the weak; there were few who mourned his passing, except those to whom he owed money.

Alan Bond

They were Australia's folk king and queen. He was the embodiment of the Australian dream, the true to life rags-to-riches entrepreneur who became a hero to the people after bringing his country glory by winning the prestigious yachting trophy, the America's Cup. At the height of his reign of power in the mid-1980s he was worth nearly £1 billion.

But in 1991 Alan Bond, Australia's answer to Donald Trump, faced bankruptcy court and claimed he had almost nothing left of his fortune. It was the ultimate tale of the multi-millionaire who lived his life to excess, then lost everything when the public's love and admiration turned to envy and mistrust.

Bond was born in 1938 in London and moved with his family to Australia eleven years later. He left school at the age of fifteen because he felt he wasn't being challenged, and took up signpainting as a profession. His goal was to be a millionaire at twenty-one. And he was. At seventeen he married Eileen (her nickname was Red), the daughter of a wool broker named Doozer Hughes. Bond took a loan out from his father-in-law and bought a piece of land in the hills of Perth, on the western coast of Australia. A land boom in the late Sixties left Bond a wealthy man and started him on his way to becoming a millionaire.

"Red" and "Bondy" were a fun-loving, eccentric and attention-grabbing couple who became notorious for their extravagance. In 1987 Bond purchased Van Gogh's Irises at Sotheby's for £30.2 million, which at the time was the largest sum ever paid for a painting. Bond made the purchase anonymously, arousing curiosity as to who the wealthy new owner could be. It was all part of the game, however. And part of Bond's strategy of making out-rageous purchases to make people (most importantly bankers) think he was fabulously wealthy.

In truth, Bond's empire was built almost entirely on debts. Early on he adopted the method of financing deals with loans on the equity of his last purchase. In fact, after his much-publicized purchase of Irises, it was revealed that Sotheby's had lent Bond £16 million to purchase the painting, using it as collateral, and that he couldn't repay the money. Eventually, Sotheby's took the painting back. At the height of his success he owned sixty per cent of Australia's television stations, and nearly half the country's beer supply, as well as oil wells, satellites, newspapers and dirigibles (zeppelins). Add to this an entire English village, two private islands, two yachts, ten homes, 95,000 sheep,

10,000 cattle and 300 paintings and one has an idea of the kind of wealth Bond possessed. His wife, Red, would jet off to Singapore on shopping trips after lunch, swathed in diamonds from Bondy's mine.

Bond's charm and great salesmanship were a huge asset in his business dealings. It was said he could sell the cross of St Peter's basilica and persuade the Pope to go along with the deal. Australians gazed at the Bonds with a mixture of despair and affection. To many, Alan Bond was a hero. Especially after he brought the country fame and glory when he won the America's Cup yachting race after his fourth try – a prize that had never been captured by a non-American before.

Besides being a fiercely competitive sportsman, Bond was a shrewd businessman and he knew that a victory in the America's Cup would bring him, in addition to notoriety and respectability, a guarantee on the £20 million in loans he'd taken out from the banks for his most ambitious project to date. Bond was planning on building an entire city – complete with three universities – among the barren sand dunes about thirty miles from Perth. He used the America's Cup as a focal point for his new project, and built a harbour and yacht, the Southern Cross, in his new city.

In 1974, just before Bond's first challenge, the property market in Australia collapsed and the banks wanted their money back. But with Bond being featured in the newspapers every day as Australia's latest sporting celebrity, the banks decided that the political backlash of putting Bond out of business wasn't worth it. "I am going to keep belting away at whoever and whatever stands between us and the cup," he said at the time. In 1983 Bond finally won the America's Cup and became an international celebrity. In Australia he became a god – Prime Minister Bob Hawke wept when he announced his victory on national television. Many wanted to see Bond knighted, and he received the Order of Australia. A mini-series based on Bondy and Red, The Challenge, was created.

Catastrophes

Fortunately for Bond, shortly after his America's Cup victory, banking deregulation began in Australia and the Labour government floated the Australian dollar, making money easier to obtain. Bond went on a spending spree, paying A$1 billion for a major brewery, Castlemaine Tooheys, the largest amount paid for an Australian company at the time. He then purchased the country's most popular television network, Channel Nine, for £600 million, and announced plans to build Bond University. By 1989, Bond owed £4.3 billion and was considered Australia's second richest man.

The old saying "What goes around, comes around", soon came to haunt Bond after he helped topple his old nemesis and competitor Robert Holmes à Court by buying out his controlling shares in his holding company, the Bell Group. When Bond was obliged by the federal government to shoulder Bell's debts as well, Australia's "King" of finance nearly went under. It was when he allegedly stabbed his old friend Lonrho Chief Executive Tiny Rowlands in the back by attempting to buy out controlling interest in his company without his knowledge, that Bond dug his own grave. Rowlands, a fierce British competitor, proceeded to publish a ninety-three-page report titled "The Bond Group of Companies: A Financial Analysis by Lonrho Plc", which proceeded to completely destroy Bond's credibility.

The document stated that Bond's companies were technically insolvent and maintained that they were worth about half of what its owner claimed. It also proposed that its debts were three times Bond's figure and that its profits were non-existent. "An investment in Bond Group Companies has been a disaster," it declared. Bond did his best to dismiss the report, calling it rubbish. But the Australian public were not so charmed by him anymore, especially since he had failed to win the America's Cup the year before.

It was feeding time on the Bonds. They made the list of "The 100 Most Appalling People in Australia". Soon Bond's stock prices began to drop and the media joined in on the negative campaign; newspapers ran regular series titled "Bond on the Ropes"; other headlines read "Bond Under the Hammer". He declared there was a conspiracy against him, but still began selling off his companies. He sold Kerry Packer his television network for $85 million in 1990 – the same company he bought off Packer for $450 million three years before. Since then, Bond Brewing has gone into receivership and American creditors have begun legal proceedings in Australia seeking repayment of £281 million worth of debentures. He's been doing his best to stave off bankruptcy. At the time of the stock market crash in October 1987, Alan Bond was believed to be the richest man in Australia with assets of nearly £1 billion.

In September 1991, he was ordered by the courts to repay bank loans of £140 million, believed to be the largest judgement against an individual in Australian legal history. Since then, he and Red have split. And on 14 April 1992, Bond's life of spending finally caught up to him: he was declared bankrupt by Australian courts. His lifestyle will have to undergo great changes. He is not allowed to own a car worth more than £1,100, the luxurious furnishings in his house must be sold, and he cannot apply for credit of more than £230 unless he declares his bankruptcy. He is restricted from becoming a director or manager of a company and must surrender his passport. The only thing Bond will be allowed to keep is his wardrobe full of custom-made suits. But Bond promises a comeback, and he's looking for investors ...

Freddie Laker

Sir Freddie Laker was a British folk hero who worked his way up from sweeping airplane hangers at the age of fifteen, to starting his own airline, Skytrain, a no-frills daily service from London to New York. Many say his airline was blown out of the sky by jealous competitors, and in 1982 the company collapsed in a pile of debts. For Sir Freddie it was the death of a long-standing dream.

He was knighted in 1978, at the height of his success with his airline, which offered cheap trans-Atlantic flights and opened up America for thousands of Britons. Laker Airways went belly up in February 1982 owing £270 million. Sir Freddie, who was considered the pioneer of cheap air travel, fought valiantly to save his airline, but after months of negotiations the rescue attempt failed. The announcement that the ten-year-old airline consisting of seventeen aircraft was going under, left passengers and holiday-makers stranded all over the world, and some Skytrain aircraft leaving Britain were recalled in mid-flight.

The public support for Sir Freddie was tremendous; a "Save Laker" fund was started and people called him asking where they could send money and what they could do to help: thousands of pounds were sent in. He was a passionate believer in the idea of setting up a cheap and easily available air network for everyone, and the people liked and respected him for this. His was the classic rags-to-riches story, which unfortunately ended in rags.

The son of a scrap dealer and a cleaning woman, Laker started his first business at the age of twenty-six — when he opened an aircraft spare parts company based on his savings of £240. An investment of £38,000 by a Scottish banker let the young entrepreneur expand into buying a dozen Halton aircraft (converted Halifax bombers). Later these aircraft helped get supplies into Berlin when it was under a Soviet blockade, and Aviation Traders was subsequently responsible for nearly twelve per cent of the food the city dwellers received over the next thirteen months. Even then, Laker wasn't making much in the way of profit and was known for thinking big, and trusting that work would eventually come in to cover costs and make more money.

After twelve years of running the company and earning the reputation of being willing to fly anywhere, he sold the company for £800,000. Soon after, he joined the board of British United Airways and became their managing director with and annual salary of £5,000 a year. In 1965, after a public row with BUA chairman Sir Miles Wyatt, he left the company and started Laker Airways. The company started off with three planes bought with £215,000 of his savings and the rest from bank loans.

When Laker tried to move into the trans-Atlantic market, however, he ran into opposition from aviation authorities as well as other carriers. Before Skytrain began its flights in 1977, British Airways, TWA and Pan Am were secretly meeting to plan his downfall. After a five-year fight, Sir Freddie had gained enough public backing so that Skytrain was born. His idea was to operate an air service that was much like a train, where people only had to turn up at the airport without booking and could take off at a cheap fare. He was finally given permission by the US Department of Transportation in June 1977 to undercut the cheapest trans-Atlantic fares by at least £80. When he received this approval, Air India, Iran Air and El Al — all airlines which operate between London and New York — joined in with the other airlines in a series of secret meetings to knock Laker out of the sky.

As soon as Skytrain went into operation it was an immediate success. On the inaugural flight to Los Angeles, Laker shook hands and talked to the passengers, and they told him that without Skytrain they would never have

Catastrophes

Failed Australian media mogul Christopher
Skase was declared bankrupt in June 1991 after
his debts mounted to more than £37 million.
He was formerly chairman of the now failed
Qintex group, a media and leisure group
which collapsed soon after it failed to take
over the American film studio MGM/UA. In
1988, Skase was estimated to be worth more
than A$65 million. He was only forty-years-old
when he moved into Hollywood to add to his
empire of Australian television networks and
several luxury tourist resorts. Skase, known to
have simple tastes – unlike many of his other
millionaire Australian peers – came from
humble beginnings. The flamboyant multi-
millionaire started out as a financial journalist,
but quit his job with the Australian Financial
Review to start his own company, Qintex, in
1974. He used his A$15,000 in savings to set
up the investment company, which later
concentrated on the media, tourism resorts
and leisure, and equities and properties. Skase
was soon noted for his debonair dress sense
and workaholic nature (he regularly worked
100-hour weeks), and after his business took
off, this rather eccentric entrepreneur
purchase a yacht for A$6 million and called it
the Mirage III. He decorated it entirely in
baby blue – his favourite colour. This meant
baby blue wall-to-wall carpeting, baby blue
panelling, baby blue marble, and a baby blue
banquet table. Before his fall, Skase was eyeing
further acquisitions in the US. He had been

working in property development in Spain
when his company failed, and returned
voluntarily to Australia to face charges of two
breaches of corporate laws.

been able to afford to fly to the USA. "We treated the
people like real human beings. We didn't treat them like
cattle, we didn't treat them like passengers; we treated them
like people," said Laker at the time.

On a high, he borrowed hundreds of millions of dollars
to buy new aircraft for his fleet and run a European Skytrain
service he was planning. A year after Laker launched
Skytrain, he was awarded a knighthood – the greatest
symbol of acceptance he could have achieved. The ex-Prime
Minister Margaret Thatcher was one of his biggest backers
and fans. But eventually the opposition from the major
airlines and the recession defeated him, and his loans turned
into heavy burdens when interest rates rose and the
exchange rate plummeted. The final blow was given when
Pan Am lowered its prices to match those of Laker's fleet.
Laker Airways collapsed on 5 February 1982. In August
1985 he accepted an $8 million peace offer from British
Airways and other airlines who he accused of allegedly
conspiring to put him out of business and prevent him from
starting up again. This cleared the way for the privatization
of BA.

Since the failure of Laker Airways, Sir Freddie has tried
his hand at running a package tour operation, inventing a
magnetic game for passengers to play with on flights, and,
at the age of seventy, he has recently started Laker Airways
again with the aim of flying holiday-makers between the
United States and the Bahamas at cheap rates and eventually moving back into the British/American market
operating low-cost trans-Atlantic flights.

Catastrophes

Once as patriotic as they come, Laker now says he avoids Britain like the plague: "The way I was treated by the government and the British travel trade, I don't owe England a thing. The country would have to change a hell of a lot for me to want to go galloping back there. I'm appreciated here in America. The Brits don't appreciate anyone."

Ivar Kreuger

Swedish born millionaire Ivar Kreuger was known as the "Match King" and once owned the world's largest monopoly. During the 1920s he was sole owner or controlled the supply of three-quarters of the world's matches. But just a few years later, Kreuger killed himself with a pistol, with little left of his $650 million fortune after squandering or losing most of it.

Kreuger was trained as an engineer in his native Sweden, then travelled the world before returning there to start a construction company. He soon became successful and began building throughout Europe, then branched out into banking and film financing. After finding that he could get supplies of phosphorous and potash for the manufacturing of matches, when others could not, he decided to go into the business and in 1915 he started his own match company.

By 1917 he was raking in the profits, had taken over his competitors and was in control of the Swedish match industry. Eventually he moved into France, Yugoslavia, Turkey, Eastern Europe, and South and Central America where he also monopolized the industry. Kreuger was an eccentric businessman, however, and took to compulsively layering his empire with mysterious companies where he could launder funds. He always had a great deal for the investor, with higher interest than anyone else could offer, and when rumours surfaced that Kreuger was having problems with his businesses, he would purposely overpay his taxes by $150,000 to make others think he was still a very wealthy man. As Robert Maxwell later did, Kreuger would pretend to take phone calls from world leaders such as Stalin, to impress his waiting visitors. He began putting together more and more deals, but his companies weren't making enough money to pay the huge dividends he promised, so the "Match King" began forging notes. One note he forged from the Italian government was for $143 million.

In 1931, Kreuger suffered a stroke, presumably caused by the incredible stress he was feeling by trying to juggle his fraudulent deals. Finally, on 12 March 1932, he put an end to his life with a shotgun. Although he considered himself a ruined man, he was still worth $200 million at the time of his death — despite squandering hundreds of millions of dollars and losing a hundred million more.

Titles in the World Famous series

World Famous Cults and Fanatics

World Famous Scandals

World Famous Strange Tales and Weird Mysteries

World Famous Crimes of Passion

World Famous Unsolved Crimes

World Famous Catastrophes

Future titles
in the World Famous series

World Famous Strange but True

World Famous True Ghost Stories

World Famous Gangsters

World Famous Robberies

World Famous Weird News Stories

World Famous SAS and Elite Forces

World Famous Royal Scandals

World Famous UFOs

World Famous Unsolved

World Famous War Heroes

World Famous True Love Stories

World Famous Spies